CENTENARY EXHIBITION

CENTENARY EXHIBITION

September 24, 1896–September 24, 1996

The Matthew J. and Arlyn Bruccoli Collection
The Thomas Cooper Library

University of South Carolina Press for
The Thomas Cooper Library

813.5
Fitzgerald

© 1996 University of South Carolina

Published in Columbia, South Carolina, by the
University of South Carolina Press

Manufactured in the United States of America

00 99 98 97 96   5 4 3 2 1

Library of Congress Cataloging-in-Publication Data

Thomas Cooper Library.
  F. Scott Fitzgerald : September 24, 1896–September 24, 1996 : centenary exhibition : the Matthew J. and Arlyn Bruccoli Collection, the Thomas Cooper Library.
    p. cm.
ISBN 1-57003-150-9
1. Fitzgerald, F. Scott (Francis Scott),
1896–1940—Authorship—Exhibitions.
2. Authors and publishers—United States—History—
20th century—Exhibitions.
3. Authorship—Exhibitions.
I. Bruccoli, Matthew Joseph, 1931–   . II. Bruccoli, Arlyn.
III. Title.
PS3511.I9Z874 1996
813'.52—dc20   96-10075

For Scottie
and
For Arlyn

*The problem of the
professional writer is
not identical with that
of the literary artist;
but when a literary artist
is also a professional writer,
he cannot solve the problems
of the one function without
reference to the other.*

—William Charvat, *The Profession of
Authorship in America, 1800–1870*

Contents

Foreword   8

Preface   9

I   "Swimming Under Water": Fitzgerald and the Writing Trade   *Michael Cody*   11

II   Author and Publisher: "Radical Writer" in an "Ultra-conservative House"   *Mary Sidney Watson*   21

III   "The Metamorphosis of Amateur into Professional": Entering Short-Story Markets   *Tracy Simmons Bitonti*   35

IV   "Each Time in a New Disguise": The Author as a Commercial Magazinist   *Park Bucker*   47

V   An American Man of Letters   *Robert F. Moss*   59

color photo section   *following page* 64

VI   The Hollywood Years, 1937–1940   *Cy League*   73

VII   Second Act: Revival and Restoration   *Catherine E. Lewis*   85

Supplementary Display Cases   *Robert W. Trogdon*   97

Wall Display: Graniteville Room   *Robert W. Trogdon*   99

Apprenticeship   *Robert W. Trogdon*   101

Zelda Fitzgerald   *Robert W. Trogdon and Tracy Simmons Bitonti*   103

Scripts Based on Fitzgerald's Works   *Paul D. Schultz*   105

Scottie Fitzgerald, 1921–1986   *M.J.B.*   106

Primary Bibliography   108

Secondary Bibliography   110

Foreword

In 1994 the University of South Carolina became the proud recipient of the Matthew J. and Arlyn Bruccoli Collection of F. Scott Fitzgerald. The acquisition of this research archive—which embraces American culture between the World Wars—brought immediate attention to the University of South Carolina and established the Thomas Cooper Library as a major repository for special collections of modern American literature. As anticipated at the time of its acquisition, the Bruccoli-Fitzgerald collection is attracting other important collections to the University.

I find it difficult adequately to express the pride we have in being the home for one of the most comprehensive research collections of modern literature in the United States. It was built as a working collection for the use of students and researchers. Its permanent preservation at the Thomas Cooper Library facilitates the usability of the material for as long as American literature matters. This catalogue and the accompanying exhibition are just two of the fruits harvested from this abundant collection. In addition to the importance of acquiring this impressive collection, an equally meaningful achievement of the Thomas Cooper Library was the solidification of a close relationship of support and enthusiasm from Arlyn and Matthew J. Bruccoli—which provides a pattern for future relationships between the Thomas Cooper Library and collectors.

George Terry
Vice Provost and Dean for Libraries and Information Systems

Preface

The Exhibition   This exhibition catalogue was compiled by the members of my English 840D at the University of South Carolina. Each of the seven students in the seminar selected an aspect of F. Scott Fitzgerald's career that could be documented with material from the Bruccoli Collection at the Thomas Cooper Library, University of South Carolina. The rationale for the exhibition and the catalogue has been to use the physical evidence from a writer's publications and related activities to construct literary history in accordance with William Charvat's explication of the profession of authorship. The descriptive sections for the seven units are supplemented by lists of exhibited items selected by the curator of the collection. All the material is drawn from one collection; no items have been borrowed from other archives. One purpose of the project is to demonstrate the utility of a private collection built by a scholar-collector. The catalogue also provides a response to questions raised by non-specialists: What use are rare books and manuscripts? What do you do with them? In the hands of a competent collector there are no "mere collector's items." Every piece has utility as part of the archive. Literary bibliography is literary history.

The Collection   The Matthew J. and Arlyn Bruccoli Collection of F. Scott Fitzgerald became a serious endeavor after we married in 1957. My initial plan was to assemble a working collection for Fitzgerald research culminating in a descriptive bibliography; but the collection inexorably grew to encompass Fitzgerald's literary world. John Cook Wyllie, Curator of Rare Books at The University of Virginia, was my earliest encourager and best mentor.

The endeavor intensified after I began working with Scottie Fitzgerald in 1969—the year that I joined the University of South Carolina faculty. Our collaboration became my bibliographical festival. She was not a scholar, but she understood the purpose of my collecting. Some of the splendid items in the collection were gifts from Scottie. After her death in 1986 I became increasingly concerned about keeping the collection permanently together for the use of students, teachers, and researchers. George Terry, Vice Provost and Dean for Libraries and Information Systems, planned the gift-purchase arrangement whereby my Fitzgerald Collection and related collections were acquired by the Thomas Cooper Library.

These are some of my bookman friends who helped me: Bart Auerbach, William Cagle, C. E. Frazer Clark (especially Fraze), Charles Feinberg, Peter Keisogloff, John S. Van E. Kohn, Hyman Kritzer, Richard Layman, Charles Mann, Linton Massey, Jack Neiburg, Maurice Neville, Michael Papantonio, Anthony Rota, R. L. Samsell, Henry Wenning, Fred Zentner.

This catalogue was designed by Rebecca Blakeney. It is published with the support of Catherine Fry, Director of the University of South Carolina Press, and Dean George Terry. Production of the catalogue was abetted by Park Bucker, Robert W. Trogdon, and Judith S. Baughman.

The keepers of special collections at the Thomas Cooper Library have been entirely supportive: Roger Mortimer, Jamie S. Hansen, Patrick Scott and Paul D. Schultz.

M.J.B.

"Swimming Under Water"
Fitzgerald and the Writing Trade

by Michael Cody

"All good writing," F. Scott Fitzgerald advised his daughter, Scottie, "is *swimming under water* and holding your breath" (*Crack-Up*, p. 304). Fitzgerald's short stories and novels read as if they were the product of effortless genius, but their vivid and lyrical prose demanded intense concentration and exertion as he immersed himself in his fiction, revising and rewriting through layers of drafts.

Fitzgerald's contemporaries often judged him a careless and undisciplined writer who wrote for money and celebrity. This judgment was based in part on his magazine writing, thought of as hack work by his contemporaries, an abuse of his talent through "spilling it in little pieces," as John Dos Passos put it to Fitzgerald in an October 1936 letter (*Crack-Up*, p. 311). Fitzgerald believed that the novel form best suited his fiction, but his short stories were not second-rate work. At the height of his career as a writer for commercial magazines, Fitzgerald wrote stories such as "The Swimmers" for *The Saturday Evening Post* (October 19, 1929) with eloquence and deep feeling.

From his earliest days Fitzgerald was a self-historiographer, experiencing things fully only when he had written about them. He made lists and schedules and plans for himself and his work. He recorded his thoughts, observations, and impressions in the notebooks he kept throughout his life. In 1940 he gave this advice to Sheilah Graham, his companion in Hollywood:

> You must begin by making notes. You may have to make notes for years.... When you think of something, when you recall something, put it ... down when you think of it. You may never recapture it quite as vividly the second time. (*Beloved Infidel*, p. 315)

As he declared in "One Hundred False Starts," Fitzgerald drew his material from his own experiences: "Whether it's something that happened twenty years ago or only yesterday, I must start out with an emotion—one that's close to me and that I can understand" (*Afternoon of an Author*, p. 132). His genius lay in his ability to capture what he felt, to transfer it to a character or a situation, locate it in a particular time, surround it with a sense of place and atmosphere, to give it life through words.

He wrote his first drafts with a soft pencil on unlined legal-sized sheets. When satisfied with the basics of a story, he gave the manuscript to a typist who returned to him a triple-spaced typescript, usually with two carbons. The triple spacing allowed room for his inevitable extensive revisions. Fitzgerald generally tried to work on one of the carbons, transferring his additions and deletions from it to the ribbon copy. But his reworking was often so extensive that it required both carbons as well as the original. Corrections and changes were then given back to the typist. This part of Fitzgerald's writing process continued until there was a "finished" typescript.

With his novels the interval between the mailing of the typescript to Scribners and the return of the galley proofs gave Fitzgerald time to rethink what he had written. The galleys then became the next draft to be revised. Fitzgerald so extensively rewrote *The Great Gatsby* in galley proofs that they had to be reset, and it was not until this stage of revision that the form and language of the novel became fully realized.

When revising, Fitzgerald focused extensively on the basics: words and sentences. He replaced one word with a better word, sharpening an image. He adjusted the phrasing of sentences, smoothing the rhythms of his prose. It is likely that Fitzgerald wrote by ear, hearing the words and sentences before he wrote them down. His painstaking concentration on the stylistic details of his manuscripts, typescripts, and galley proofs was an intense struggle to bring to life his internal authorial voice.

Fitzgerald not only knew how the prose should sound but also knew, as he wrote in "How to Waste Material," that his fiction must be "purified by an incorruptible style and by the catharsis of a passionate emotion" (*Afternoon of an Author,* p. 120). He developed his subjects with genius and passion, but many critics took him to task for dealing too often with the young, beautiful, and wealthy, no matter what his themes or the fates of his characters. Fitzgerald defended himself in the introduction he wrote for the 1934 Modern Library edition of *The Great Gatsby:*

> Reading it over one can see how it could have been improved—yet without feeling guilty of any discrepancy from the truth, as far as I saw it; truth or rather the *equivalent* of the truth, the attempt at honesty of imagination. I had just re-read Conrad's preface to *The Nigger,* and I had recently been kidded half haywire by critics who felt that my material was such as to preclude all dealing with mature persons in a mature world. But my God! it was my material, and it was all I had to deal with. (*In His Own Time,* p. 156)

But his literary sensibilities extended beyond his own work. He had an innate sense of what good writing should be. He recognized Hemingway's talent. He praised and criticized Thomas Wolfe. His letters to his contemporaries, to young writers, and to critics are filled with literary opinions and advice.

Fitzgerald read widely all his life and made penetrating assessments of writers' works and ideas. He often attempted to imitate in prose John Keats's poetic rhythms and rich imagery. Joseph Conrad influenced his ideas about the purpose of fiction, that the "essential reaction" to it "shall be profound and enduring" (*Life in Letters,* p. 252). Fitzgerald approached his own work with a belief in his place among the great writers who had come before him, an understanding that each short story and novel he wrote stood as the end point of a tangible and active literary tradition.

❖ ❖ ❖

1. Fitzgerald's copy of Samuel Butler's *Notebooks* (New York: Dutton, 1917), inscribed by Fitzgerald on free front endpaper and annotated throughout.

1917, the first date in Fitzgerald's inscription, was the last year he spent at Princeton and a year in which he wrote apprentice works important to his career. Some pieces would become his first commercial publications; some would be adapted for *This Side of Paradise*. Two years later, in an September 18, 1919, letter to Maxwell Perkins acknowledging Scribners' acceptance of *This Side of Paradise*, Fitzgerald proclaimed that every young writer ought to read Butler's *Notebooks*. His admiration for the work endured. In 1923 he placed it at the top of a list of those books he considered the best he had read. When Fitzgerald began organizing his own *Notebooks*, probably some time in 1932, he tried to emulate Butler.

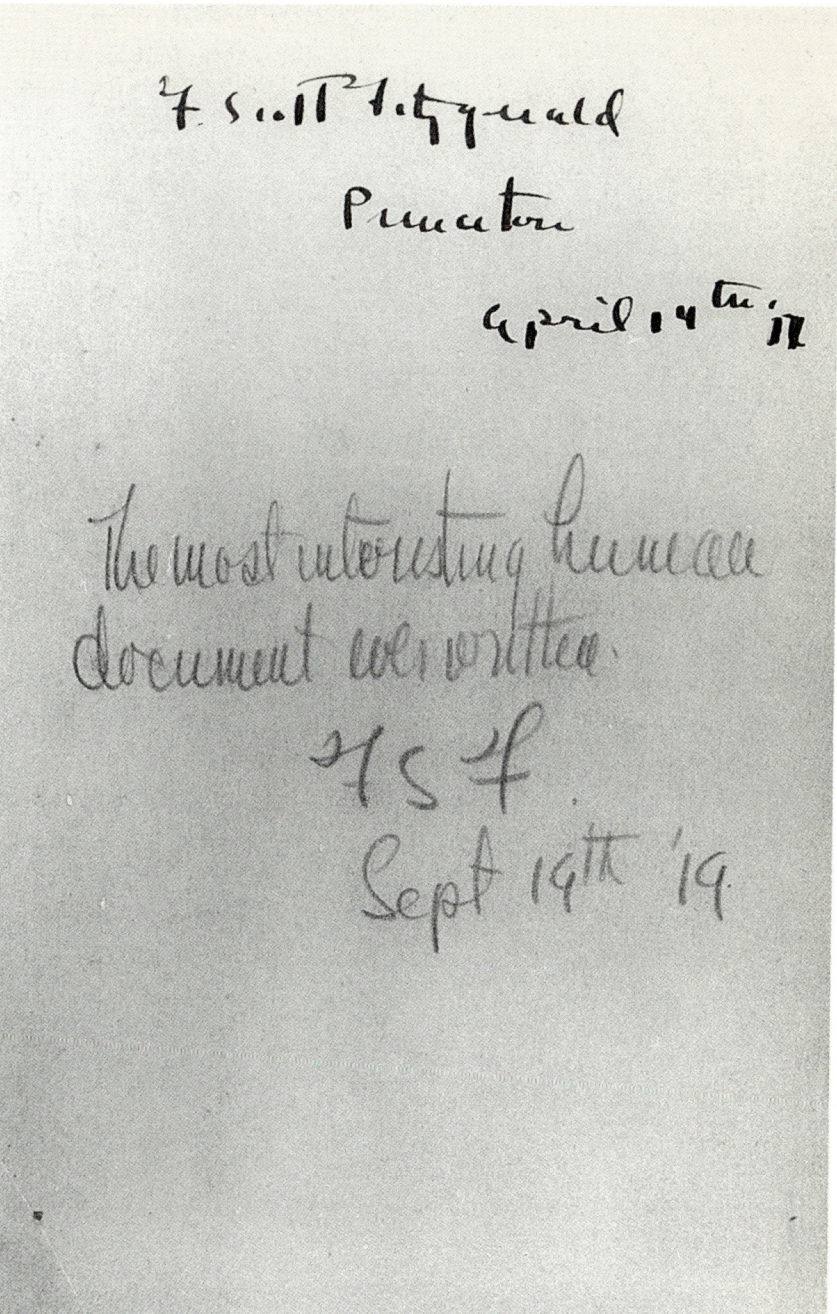

2. Fitzgerald's rejected Preface to *This Side of Paradise* (New York: Scribners, 1920), CC, 2 pp. (see item 15); Gordon Bryant's 1920 portrait of Fitzgerald inscribed to Stephan Parrott.

Fitzgerald's Preface to *This Side of Paradise* was not used when Scribners published the novel on March 26, 1920, but was published separately in 1975. This version of the Preface was included in a carbon copy of the beginning of *This Side of Paradise* that Fitzgerald sent to Stephan Parrott, probably in fall 1919. The two met when they were students together at the Newman School in Hackensack, New Jersey. Their friendship was based on their putative brotherhood as protégés of Father Cyril Sigourney Webster Fay, the model for Monsignor Darcy in *This Side of Paradise*.

```
                    Preface.
          Two years ago when I was a very young man indeed, I had
urge, unmistakable urge to write a book. It was to be a picturesque
novel, original in form and alternating a melancholy, naturalistic
egotism with a picture of the generation then hastening to war.
          It was to be naive in places, shocking in others, painful
to the conventional and not without it's touch of ironic sublimity.
The "leading character", a loiterer on the borderland of genius,
loved many women, and gazed at himself in many mirrors - in fact,
women and mirrors were preponderant on all the important pages.
          I completed it during the last gasp of a last year at
college, and the intricasies of a training camp. It's epigrams
were polished by the substitution of the word one for the word you;
it's chapter titles were phrased to sound somewhat like lines from
Pre-Raphaelite poems, somewhat like the electric signs over musical
comedies; the book itself was a tedius casserole of a dozen by
McKenzie, Wells and Robert Hugh Benson, largely flavored by the
great undigested butter-ball of Dorian Gray.
          The conservative publisher to whom I sent it kept it for
several months and finally returned it with the complaint that the
hero failed in the end to find himself, and that this defection
would so certainly disappoint the reader as to predestine the book
to failure.
          He suggested that I remedy this defect and I pondered the
difficulty for several weeks - how I could intrigue the hero into
a "philosophy of life" when my own ideas were in much the state of
Alice's after the hatter's tea-party.
          At length I took a tip from Schoepenhaur, Hugh Walpole
and even the early Wells - begged the question by plunging boldly
into obscurity; astounded myself with an unpenetrable chapter where
I left the hero alone with rhapsodic winds and super-significant
stars -; gemmed the paragraphs with neo-symbolic bits culled from
my own dismantled poems - such awe-inspiring half-lines as
          * * * * the dark celibacy of greatness * * * Youth, the
Queen Anne Clavichord from which age wrings the symphony of art * * *
the tired pitying beauty of monotony which hung like summer air over
the gate to his soul * * *
          And finding that I had merely dragged the hero from a
logical muddle into an illogical one, I dispatched him to the war
and callously slew him several thousand feet in the air, whence he
fell "not like a dead bird, but as a splendid life-bound swallow
* * * * down * * * * down * * * * "
          The book finished with four dots - there was a fifth dot
but I erased it.
          After two months it was again refused. The conservative
publisher was, however, optimistic enough to send it to a more
radical competitor, who specialized in leading out the new Slavic
novelists and giving free air to experiments in Celtic phrasing.
This publisher did not even faintly consider it.
```

---

3. "Babes in the Woods," *Nassau Literary Magazine* **(May 1917);** *This Side of Paradise* **(New York: Scribners, 1920).**

In 1917 Fitzgerald wrote several pieces that would form a bridge between the writing of his apprenticeship and that of his professional career. After its publication in Princeton's *Nassau Lit*, "Babes in the Woods" became Fitzgerald's first commercial story sale (*The Smart Set*, September 1919) and was adapted for the "Isabelle" subchapter of *This Side of Paradise*.

4. Fitzgerald to Dr. Frank H. Vizetelly, c. 1922, St. Paul, Minn., ALS, 1 p.

Fitzgerald wrote this letter to Dr. Vizetelly, editor of the Funk and Wagnalls *Standard Dictionary,* to provide an explication for Bilphism, the religion espoused by Gloria's mother in *The Beautiful and Damned.*

5. *The Vegetable* (New York: Scribners, 1923), inscribed to Ernest Truex on free front endpaper; 1923 Sam H. Harris contract for the play's production.

Fitzgerald's early interest in the stage, both in St. Paul and at Princeton, led to the only play of his professional career, *The Vegetable,* written in expectation of financial rewards. Scribners published the play in book form on April 27, 1923. Sam H. Harris agreed to produce *The Vegetable,* but the play failed its Atlantic City tryout in November 1923. Ernest Truex appeared in the leading role as Jerry Frost.

6. *The Great Gatsby,* unrevised galley proofs, 57 pp.

Fitzgerald had several tentative titles for the novel that would finally be known as *The Great Gatsby*. Trimalchio is the name of the wealthy and ostentatious party-giver in *The Satyricon*, Petronius's satirical portrait of early Rome. Other tentative titles included "Trimalchio in West Egg," "Gold-Hatted Gatsby," and "The High-Bouncing Lover," the latter two adapted from the novel's epigraph: "Then wear the gold hat, if that will move her;/If you can bounce high, bounce for her too,/Till she cry 'Lover, gold-hatted, high-bouncing lover,/I must have you!'" Fitzgerald, acting on advice from Maxwell Perkins, revised and restructured the novel in the galleys, bringing it to its final brilliance. This is the only located unmarked set of original galleys. The handwritten title change is not in Fitzgerald's hand.

The Great Gatsby

Gal. 1—Fitzgerald's Trimalchio—46725—12-12-31

CHAPTER I

IN my younger and more vulnerable years my father told me something that I've been turning over in my mind ever since.

"When you feel like criticising any one," he said, "just remember that everybody in this world hasn't had the advantages that you've had."

He didn't say any more, but we've always been unusually communicative in a reserved way, and I understood that he meant a great deal more than that. In consequence, I'm inclined to reserve all judgments, a habit that has opened up many curious natures to me and also made me the victim of not a few veteran bores. The abnormal mind is quick to detect and attach itself to this quality when it appears in a normal person, and so it came about that in college I was unjustly accused of being a politician, because I was privy to the secret griefs of wild, unknown men. Most of the confidences were unsought—frequently I have feigned sleep, preoccupation, or a hostile levity when I realized by some unmistakable sign that an intimate revelation was quivering on the horizon; for the intimate revelations of young men, or at least the terms in which they express them, are usually plagiaristic and marred by obvious suppressions. Reserving judgments is a matter of infinite hope. I am still a little afraid of missing something if I forget that, as my father snobbishly suggested, and I snobbishly repeat, a sense of the fundamental decencies is parcelled out unequally at birth.

And, after boasting this way of my tolerance, I come to the admission that it has a limit. Conduct may be founded on the hard rock or the wet marshes, but after a certain point I don't care what it's founded on. When I came back from the East last autumn I felt that I wanted the world to be in uniform and at a sort of moral attention forever; I wanted no more riotous excursions with privileged glimpses into the human heart. It was only Gatsby, the man who gives his name to this book, that was exempted from my reaction. Gatsby, who represented everything for which I have an unaffected scorn. If personality is an unbroken series of successful gestures, then there was something gorgeous about him, some heightened sensitivity to the

7. Coda to "The Swimmers," *Saturday Evening Post* (October 19, 1929), RTS, 45 pp.

This revised ending of "The Swimmers" reveals the effort Fitzgerald expended on a crucial step in his writing process: the careful revision of his typescript drafts. His revisions demonstrate how his expatriate experience reinforced his deeply felt identification with America, with its history and hopes. "The Swimmers" was a story for *The Saturday Evening Post*, but the emotion and painstaking revision evident here is not the work of a writer interested only in quick financial gain.

-46-

passenger was through at the window. When she turned they both started; he saw it was the girl.

"Oh, hello," she cried " I'm glad you're going. I was just asking when the pool opened. The great thing about this ship is that you can always get a swim."

"Why do you like to swim?" he demanded.

"You always ask me that." she laughed.

"Perhaps you'd tell me, if we had dinner together to-night."

But when he left her he knew that she could never tell him, she was one or another. France was a land, England was a people, but America, the graves at Shiloh and the tired, drawn, nervous faces of its great men, and the country boys dieing in the Argonne for a phrase that was empty before their bodies withered. It was a willingness of the heart.

8. "Home to Maryland" (1931), RTS, 53 pp.

"Home to Maryland" was the working title of a 1931 story that was eventually renamed "On Your Own." Seven magazines declined the story between 1931 and 1936, and it was not published until *Esquire* printed it (January 30, 1979), almost thirty-nine years after Fitzgerald's death. The typescript displays Fitzgerald's method of revision as he carefully works on words and phrases.

9. *Tender Is the Night*, unrevised galley proofs for the first installment of the *Scribner's Magazine* serialization; Fitzgerald's handwritten notes for the novel, 2 pp.

Tender Is the Night evolved through nine years and seventeen stages of composition. The text as represented by these galleys for the first *Scribner's Magazine* installment (January 1934) was not the final form of the novel Scribners published on April 12, 1934. Fitzgerald extensively revised the proofs for the magazine installments and then revised the final serialized version for the book publication of *Tender Is the Night*. The handwritten notes list the order of events in the novel, especially those in Books 1 and 2 (see item 23).

10. Fitzgerald to Gilbert Seldes, February 2, 1934, Baltimore, Md., TLS, 2 pp.

After the death of American humorist Ring Lardner in September 1933, *The New Republic* (October 11, 1933) published "Ring," Fitzgerald's tribute to Lardner, who had been his friend and the model for Abe North in *Tender Is the Night*. Maxwell Perkins then asked Fitzgerald to help edit and write the introduction for a collection of Lardner's work, but Fitzgerald declined because he felt that the project would take his attention from *Tender Is the Night*, which was in the final stages before serialization. He recommended critic Gilbert Seldes for the job. Seldes retained the title *First and Last*, and Fitzgerald was disappointed with the volume.

11. Fitzgerald's 1936 reading list for Dorothy Richardson, written in her hand.

In 1936, before he established the "College of One" for Sheilah Graham in Hollywood, Fitzgerald prepared a list of "required" readings for Dorothy Richardson, a private-duty nurse he hired while he was attempting to stop drinking during his stay at the Grove Park Inn in Asheville, N.C.

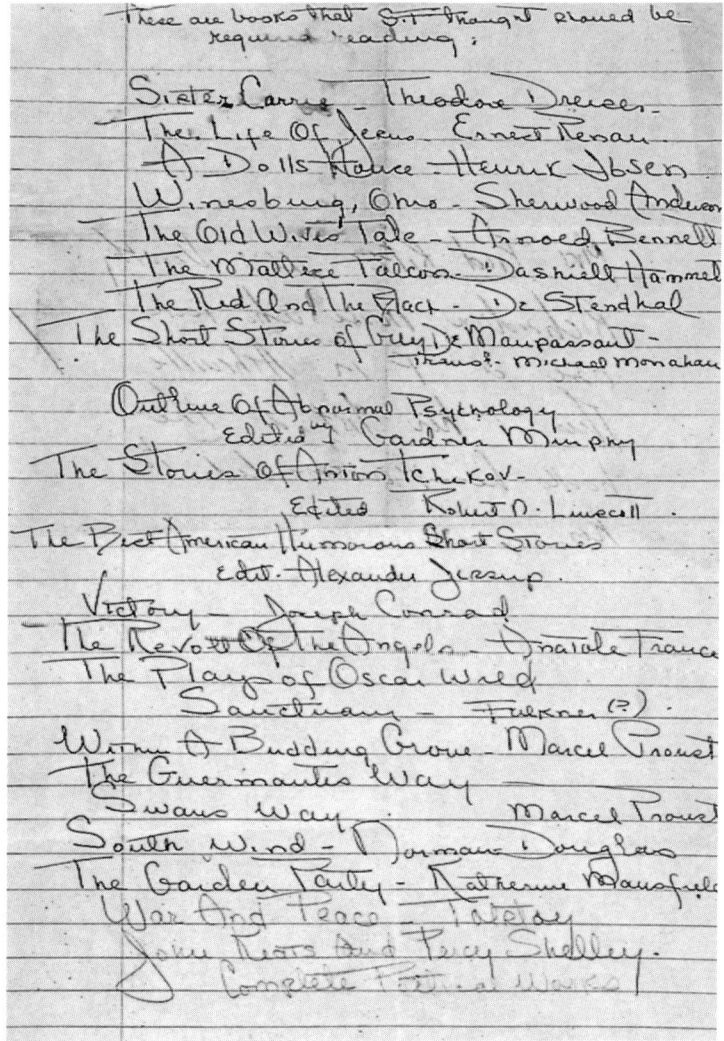

12. Fitzgerald to Robert Bennett, February 21, 1940, Encino, Calif., TLS, 1 p.; Fitzgerald to Bennett, September 25, 1940, Hollywood, Calif., TLS, 1 p.

The February 21 letter to Robert Bennett, a Los Angeles book dealer, shows that Fitzgerald read widely, since he refers to works by Plato, George Bernard Shaw, Fyodor Dostoevsky, and Rudyard Kipling. The September 25 letter also serves as evidence of Fitzgerald's affinity with John Keats, whose poems influenced Fitzgerald's use of lyrical language and his sense of the Romantic. The Keats poem referred to is "On First Looking into Chapman's Homer."

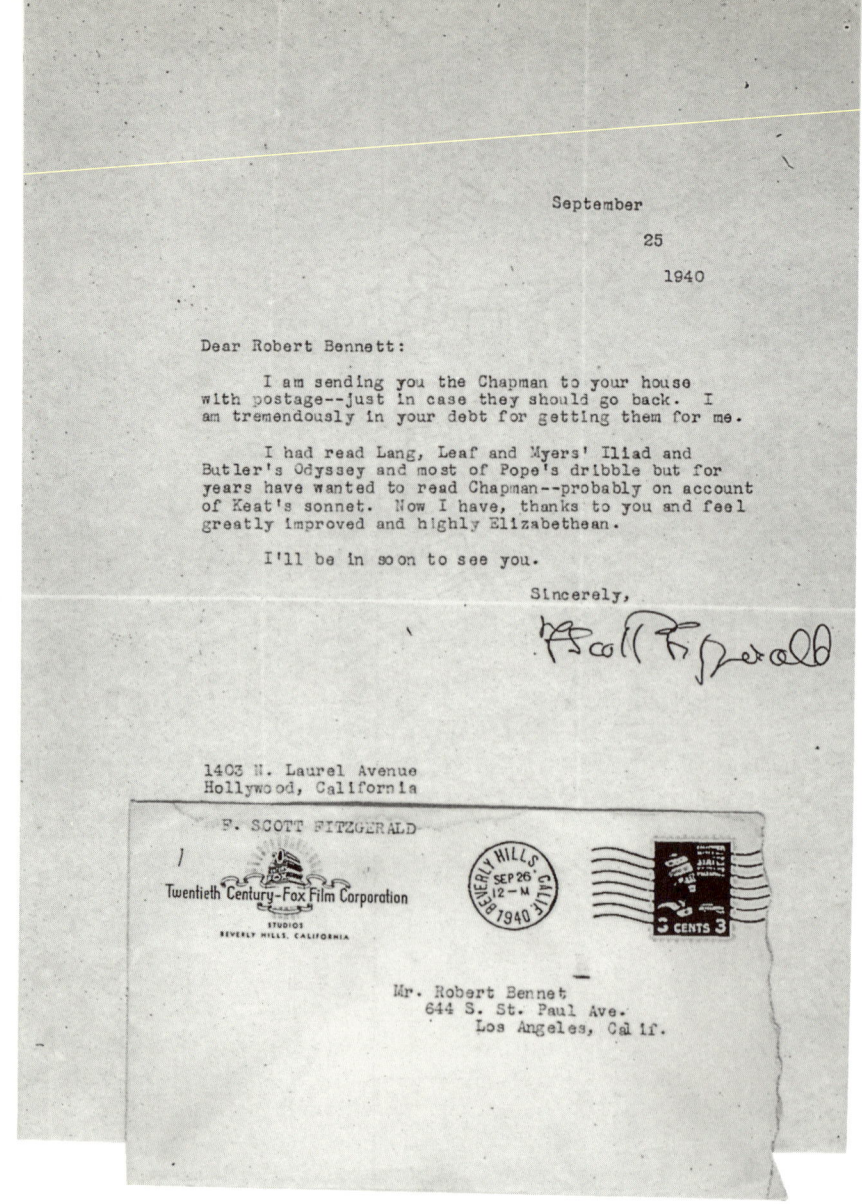

Author and Publisher
"Radical Writer" in an "Ultra-conservative House"

by Mary Sidney Watson

With the publication of F. Scott Fitzgerald's first novel, *This Side of Paradise,* on March 26, 1920, Charles Scribner's Sons became a crucial component in Fitzgerald's balancing act as both popular short-story writer and serious novelist. Scribners had a distinguished literary list, which included Henry James, Edith Wharton, Thomas Nelson Page, and Robert Louis Stevenson. Although company president Charles Scribner II initially judged Fitzgerald's novel unsuitable for his house, editor Maxwell Perkins's argument "that a publisher's first allegiance is to talent" persuaded Scribner to accept the young writer's work (Berg, p. 16). Perkins's victory brought Fitzgerald's first novel into the public eye under an imprint that gave it immediate prestige.

Scribners gained critical attention for *This Side of Paradise,* which was widely reviewed. Scribners and Maxwell Perkins were instrumental in gaining acceptance for Fitzgerald as a serious novelist, but Perkins's failure to see that the novel was properly copyedited resulted in a high number of errors in the novel and burdened Fitzgerald with a reputation as a careless writer. Although *This Side of Paradise* was a commercial success (nine printings for a total of 41,075 copies in 1920), Fitzgerald's 1920 earnings from the novel came to only $6,200 (10 percent royalty at $2.75 per copy), less than the $11,400 he earned from his short stories in magazine sales and movie rights in the same year (*Ledger*). Beginning with *Flappers and Philosophers* on September 10, 1920, Scribners followed each of Fitzgerald's novels with a collection of short stories, a standard method of the time to keep a novelist's name before the public.

The association of Fitzgerald with the youth of his time, as "flapper" writer, was a deeply ingrained aspect of his public image. Before Fitzgerald's second novel, *The Beautiful and Damned,* was published on March 4, 1922, both Fitzgerald and Perkins believed this new book required a shift to a more literary image. They also worried that the novel had been harmed by its abridged serialization in *Metropolitan Magazine. The Beautiful and Damned* was another success, though not the blockbuster Fitzgerald would have liked; Scribners printed 50,000 copies in 1922, and the novel made the *Publishers' Weekly* best-seller lists in March (tenth place), April (sixth), and May (tenth). Although Scribners had increased Fitzgerald's royalty rate to 15 percent, the $7,000 in serial rights and $15,000 in royalties were insufficient to allow Fitzgerald to end his magazine writing and concentrate only on his career as a novelist. On April 17 Perkins encouraged Fitzgerald, suggesting "the book has consolidated your position.... for our part we are backing you for a long race and are more than ever convinced that you will win it" (*Dear Scott/Dear Max,* p. 58).

Perkins's influence on Fitzgerald's writing was perhaps greatest in the revision of *The Great Gatsby,* yet it was limited to structural advice and to his customary role as literary sounding board. In a November 20, 1924, letter Perkins suggested that Fitzgerald strengthen the characterization of Gatsby and that he break up a long section of Gatsby's autobiography to avoid interrupting Nick Carraway's narrative. Although *The Great Gatsby* is now Fitzgerald's most widely read novel, its initial reception following its April 10, 1925, publication showed little promise of its future fame. Scribners advertised the novel aggressively, and the critical response was generally positive, but only about 23,000 copies of *Gatsby* were sold in 1925. Early in his career Fitzgerald had established the habit of borrowing from Scribners; the $6,261 he earned from the first printing of *Gatsby* barely paid off his borrowing against that novel.

The commercial failure of *Gatsby* was so disturbing that rumors reached Perkins that a disgruntled Fitzgerald was moving to another publisher. However, Fitzgerald reassured Perkins of his loyalty to Scribners in a June 1 letter, citing "the advantages of one publisher who backs you and not your work." Fitzgerald also noted "[t]he curious advantage to a rather radical writer in being published by what is now an ultra-conservative house" (*Life in Letters,* p. 116).

The wait for the next novel stretched over nine years as Fitzgerald struggled with financial difficulties, Zelda Fitzgerald's psychiatric problems, and the creative challenges of the novel itself. Perkins maintained a warm correspondence with Fitzgerald, reaffirming his belief in Fitzgerald's talent. By the time *Tender Is the Night* was published on April 12, 1934, Fitzgerald had become best known as a highly successful short-story writer for magazines. Scribners feared the effects of the years on the public's memory and the harsh realities of the Depression marketplace. The ad campaign for *Tender Is the Night* attempted to reaffirm Fitzgerald's reputation as a serious novelist. To introduce the novel in a dignified manner and to generate money for Fitzgerald, *Tender Is the Night* was serialized in *Scribner's Magazine,* beginning in January 1934.

Scribners issued three printings totaling slightly more than 15,000 copies of *Tender Is the Night* in spring 1934, a substantial performance during the Depression era. Fitzgerald had held high hopes for its commercial success, since he needed the income from royalties to pay off his debts. Instead, Fitzgerald's earnings from the novel totaled only $5,104.65. On October 17 Perkins had the duty of sending Fitzgerald the disappointing royalty report and discouraging his requests for further advances.

Tender Is the Night was Fitzgerald's last completed novel. When he died of a heart attack on December 21, 1940, the manuscript of his new novel was unfinished. Perkins and Scribners moved to publish *The Last Tycoon, The Great Gatsby,* and five of his stories in a memorial volume, a project which promised little financial reward for the firm.

Perkins, who died in 1947, did not see the revival of Fitzgerald's reputation in the Fifties. At least in part, the possibility of that revival lay in Fitzgerald's good fortune in signing initially with a publisher whose imprint was an assurance of quality and whose belief in the necessity of supporting a writer for "the long race" provided an area of stability in which Fitzgerald could mature as a novelist.

❖ ❖ ❖

13. Fitzgerald to Shane Leslie, December 1917, Ft. Leavenworth, Kans., ALS, 3 pp.

Expecting to be sent to battle in World War I, Fitzgerald labored in training camp at Fort Leavenworth, Kansas, to complete his first novel. Anglo-Irish author Shane Leslie, whom Fitzgerald had met while a student at the Newman School, recommended "The Romantic Egoist" to his own publisher, Charles Scribner's Sons. Although Scribners decided against the novel, the gentle rejection letter, dated August 19, 1918, and probably written by junior editor Maxwell Perkins, suggested revisions and encouraged Fitzgerald to resubmit. Fitzgerald, then stationed at Montgomery, Alabama, quickly revised and resubmitted the novel, but in October Perkins again rejected it. Despite these initial setbacks, Fitzgerald would continue to revise "The Romantic Egoist" until his efforts were rewarded with the publication of his first novel, retitled *This Side of Paradise*.

This letter to Leslie describes the unusual mix of genres in "The Romantic Egoist," which is also a distinctive feature of *This Side of Paradise*. For the title page of *This Side of Paradise* Fitzgerald chose another epigraph from Rupert Brooke, dropped the one by G. K. Chesterton, and corrected the wording in the Oscar Wilde epigraph.

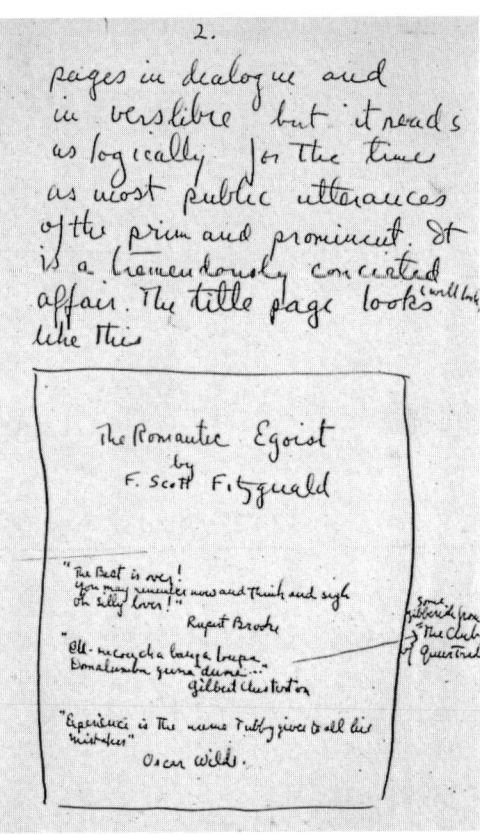

14. *This Side of Paradise* (New York: Scribners, 1920).

After his discharge from the army in February 1919, Fitzgerald temporarily shelved "The Romantic Egoist" while he worked at an ad agency in New York. In July 1919 Fitzgerald returned to his parents' home in St. Paul, determined to devote himself full time to his novel. The revised manuscript, *This Side of Paradise,* was accepted September 18, 1919, and published on March 26, 1920.

The dust-jacket flap copy touches on protagonist Amory Blaine's romances but emphasizes his moral dilemma, the "dramatic clash between the hero's desire to express himself as an artist and the pull of the deeply rooted orthodoxy within him." By focusing the description of the plot on Amory Blaine's crisis and not on the novel's depiction of the changing sexual mores among the younger generation, Scribners presented the novel as a work of literature worthy of consideration by reviewers and discerning readers. See color insert.

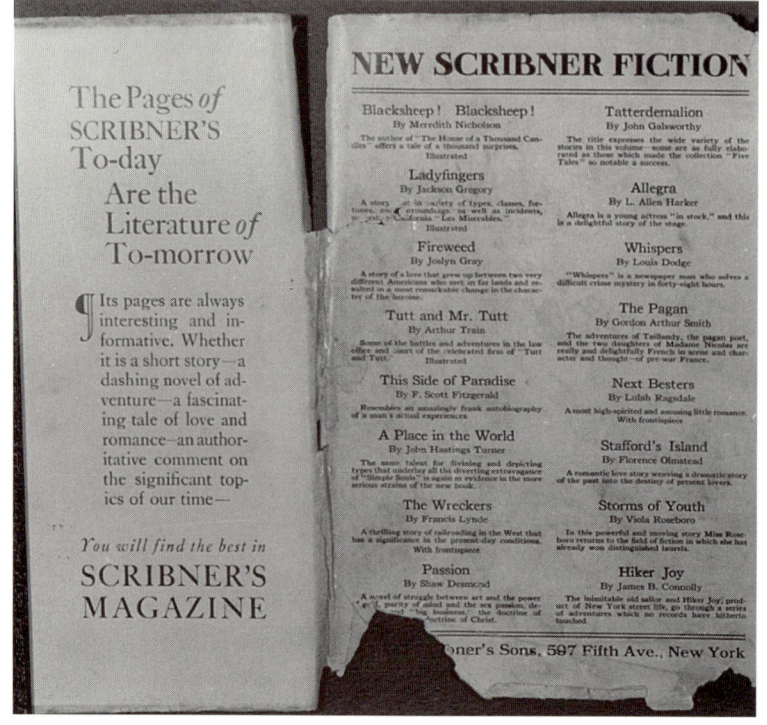

15. *This Side of Paradise,* CC, 48 pp.

The final setting-copy typescript and proofs of *This Side of Paradise* are not extant, making it impossible to determine the extent of Perkins's involvement with Fitzgerald's first novel. Although Perkins is celebrated for the extensive editorial assistance he at times gave to other writers, the correspondence between Perkins and Fitzgerald does not suggest that he contributed more than routine editing to *This Side of Paradise*. However, Fitzgerald and Perkins may have worked together on the novel in New York in November 1919.

This carbon copy (forty-eight pages of chapters 1 and 2) includes the "Author's Preface," which does not appear in the published volume (see item 2). Although large in number, the revisions between this typescript and the finished version are limited to changes in punctuation, spelling, and substitutions of single words or phrases.

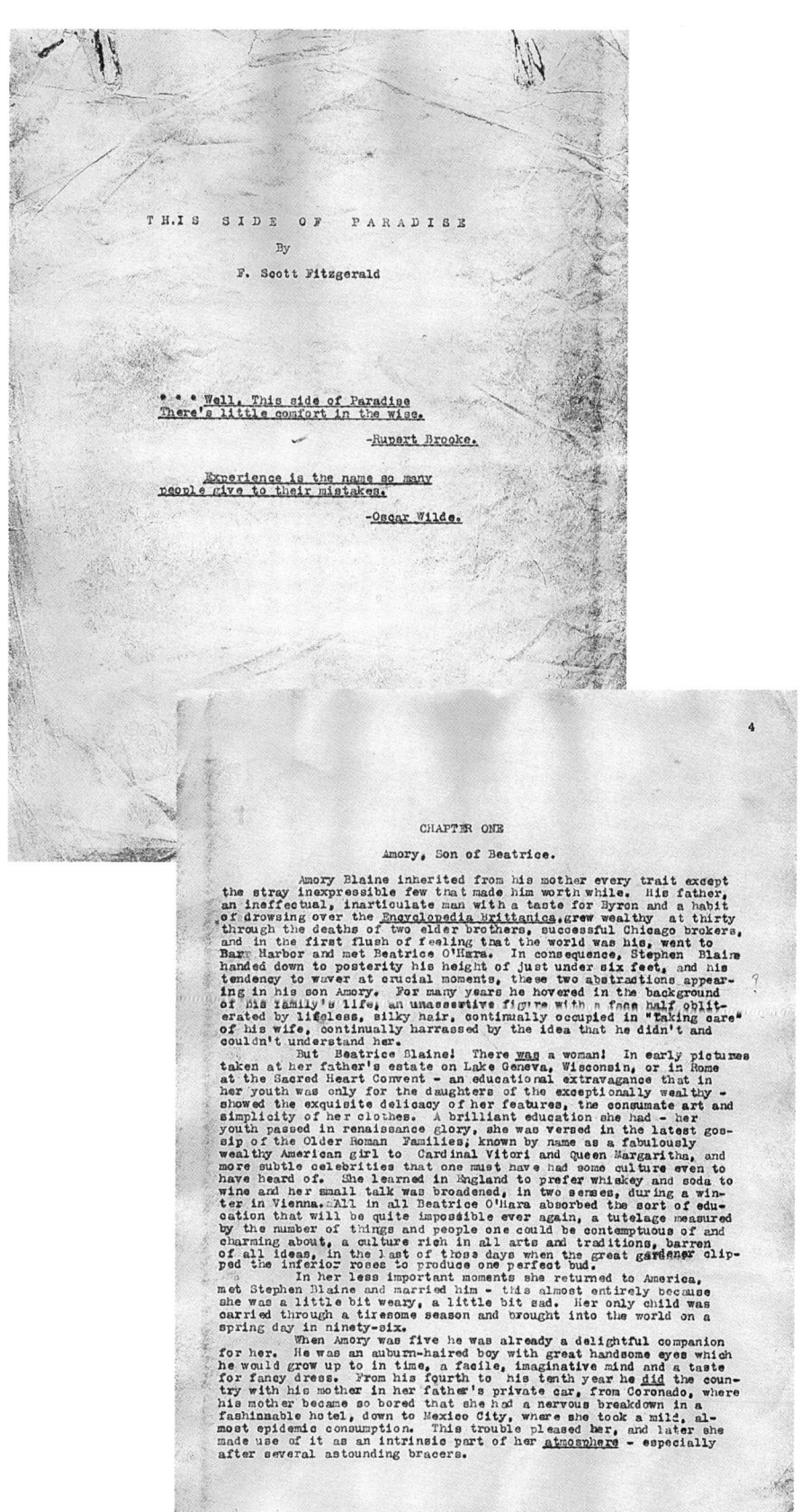

16. Fitzgerald to John Biggs, Jr., c. Winter 1921, New York City, ALS, 1 p.

This letter from Fitzgerald to his college friend and aspiring writer John Biggs, Jr. ("Jawn"), demonstrates how Fitzgerald functioned as talent scout for Scribners, to which he would bring Ernest Hemingway, Ring Lardner, and others. The postscript records Fitzgerald's appreciation of Perkins's support and editorial ability.

---

58 W. 59th St.
New York City

Dear Jawn:

Wire me today for your adress which I've mislaid. The enclosure explains why I want it.

Glad you liked my suggestion. When Perkins comes to see you I shouldn't tell him your plot but for god's sake tell him the novel's damn good! No decent workman belittles his own work unless, and until, its been over-praised.

When you finish it I have a brilliant scene for you. Let me hear from you soon

Scott F.

P.S. Perkins is one hell of a good fellow. He's the one who stuck out for my 1st novel almost 3 years ago. He's the editorial brain of the Scribner Co.

S.

P.S.² Am writing a movie for Dorothy Gish by request of Griffith for which I hope to get ten thousand.

17. *The Beautiful and Damned*, Metropolitan Magazine (September 1921).

The Beautiful and Damned ran in seven issues of *Metropolitan Magazine* (see color insert) between September 1921 and March 1922 (see item 28). Perkins feared that the distortion caused by unauthorized cuts in the serial version of what became *The Beautiful and Damned* and the "surface brilliance of the story" might cause readers to "fail to gauge its true weight and substance" (to James Branch Cabell, February 17, 1922, Scribners Archives).

The magazine's decision to feature Gloria Patch on the cover was probably designed to play on the public's interest in Fitzgerald's women, who were independent, determined, and sexually freer than most of their counterparts. Fitzgerald dropped the final paragraphs of the serial for the book publication after Zelda Fitgerald complained that it was "a piece of morality" (*Correspondence*, p. 89).

THAT exquisite heavenly irony which has tabulated the demise of many generations of sparrows seems to us to be content with the moral judgments of man upon fellow man. If there is a subtler and yet more nebulous ethic somewhere in the mind, one might believe that beneath the sordid dress and near the bruised heart of this transaction there was a motive which was not weak but only futile and sad. In the search for happiness, which search is the greatest and possibly the only crime of which we in our petty misery are capable, these two people were marked as guilty chiefly by the freshness and fullness of their desire. Their disillusion was always a comparative thing—they had sought glamor and color through their respective worlds with steadfast loyalty—sought it and it alone in kisses and in wine, sought it with the same ingenuousness in the wanton moonlight as under the cold sun of inviolate chastity. Their fault was not that they had doubted but that they had believed.

The exquisite perfection of their boredom, the delicacy of their inattention, the inexhaustibility of their discontent—were disastrous extremes—that was all. And if, before Gloria yielded up her gift of beauty, she shed one bright feather of light so that someone, gazing up from the grey earth, might say, " Look! There is an angel's wing!" perhaps she had given more than enough in exchange for her tinsel joys.

. . . The story ends here.

18. *The Beautiful and Damned* (New York: Scribners, 1922).

Published March 4, 1922, Fitzgerald's second novel, *The Beautiful and Damned*, told of the gradual deterioration of Anthony Patch, one of an affluent class of urbanites "adrift on a sea of luxury, without the anchors of homes and the rudders of responsibilities." It marks a period of Fitzgerald's career when, under the influence of *Smart Set* editors H. L. Mencken and George Jean Nathan, he was experimenting with the literary techniques of naturalism. See color insert.

> Only a few months before people had been urging him to give in, to submit to mediocrity, to go to work. But he had known that he was justified in his way of life—and he had stuck it out stanchly. Why, the very friends who had been most unkind had come to respect him, to know he had been right all along. Had not the Lacys and the Merediths and the Cartwright-Smiths called on Gloria and him at the Ritz-Carlton just a week before they sailed?
>
> Great tears stood in his eyes, and his voice was tremulous as he whispered to himself.
>
> "I showed them," he was saying. "It was a hard fight, but I didn't give up and I came through!"

TALES OF THE JAZZ AGE

BY

F. SCOTT FITZGERALD

NEW YORK
CHARLES SCRIBNER'S SONS
1922

A TABLE OF CONTENTS

MY LAST FLAPPERS

THE JELLY-BEAN . . . . Page

This is a southern story, with the scene laid in the small city of Tarleton, Georgia. I have a great affection for Tarleton, but somehow whenever I write a story about it I receive letters from all over the South denouncing me in no uncertain terms. "The Jelly-Bean," published in *The Metropolitan* drew its full share of these admonitory notes.

Of the stories included in this volume, this first one is not my favorite. It was written under strange circumstances shortly after my first novel was published, and moreover, it was the first story in which I had a collaborator. For, finding that I was unable to manage the crap-shooting episode, I turned it over to my wife, who, as a southern girl, was presumably an expert on the technique and terminology of that great sectional pastime.

THE CAMEL'S BACK . . . . Page

I suppose that of all the stories I have ever written this one cost me the least travail and perhaps gave me the most amusement. As to the labor involved, it was written during one day in the city of New Orleans, with the express purpose of buying a platinum and diamond wrist watch which cost six hundred dollars. I began it at seven in the morning, and finished it at two o'clock the same night. It was published in the *Saturday Evening Post* in 1920, and later included in the O. Henry Memorial Collection for the same year.

My amusement was derived from the fact that the camel part of the story is literally true; in fact, I have a standing engagement with the gentleman involved to attend the next fancy-dress party to which we are both invited attired as the latter part of the camel—this as a sort of atonement for being his historian.

MAY DAY . . . . Page

This somewhat unpleasant tale, published as a novelette in the *Smart Set* in June, 1920, relates a series of events which took place in the spring of the previous year. Each of the three events made a great impression upon me. In life they were unrelated, except by the general hysteria of that spring which inaugurated the Age of Jazz, but in my story I have tried, unsuccessfully I'm afraid, to weave them into a pattern—a pattern which would give the effect of those months as they appeared to at least one member of what was then the younger generation.

v

19. *Tales of the Jazz Age* (New York: Scribners, 1922), salesmen's dummy of first edition.

Scribners produced this dummy to be used by its salesmen to market the volume to booksellers. It consists of half-title, title page, table of contents, and the first sixteen pages of "The Jelly-Bean," repeated three times.

The annotated table of contents varies from the published version in story selection and the titles of two stories. The contents page of the dummy includes one story, "Two for a Cent," which does not appear in the published version, while the contents page of the book itself lists two stories, "Porcelain and Pink" and "Mr. Icky," which do not appear in the salesmen's dummy. "The Russet Witch" and "The Crusts of Love" become "O Russet Witch" and "The Lees of Happiness" in the book version. The dust jacket for *Tales of the Jazz Age* featured John Held, Jr.'s popular flappers.

---

vi   CONTENTS

FANTASIES

THE DIAMOND AS BIG AS THE RITZ . . . . Page

This first extravaganza, which appeared lastsummer in the *Smart Set*, was written utterly for my own amusement. I was in that familiar mood characterized by a perfect craving for luxury, and the story began as an attempt to feed that craving on imaginary foods.
One well-known critic has been pleased to like this story better than anything I have written. Personally I prefer "The Off Shore Pirate." But, to tamper slightly with Lincoln: "If you like this sort of thing this is the sort of thing you'll like."

THE RUSSET WITCH . . . . Page

When this was written I had just completed the first draft of my second novel, and a natural reaction made me revel in a story wherein none of the characters need be taken seriously. And I'm afraid that I was somewhat carried away by the feeling that there was no ordered scheme to which I must conform. After due consideration, however, I have decided to let it stand as it is, although the reader may find himself somewhat puzzled at the conclusion. The time element may be confusing as well. But I had best say that however the years may have dealt with Merlin Grainger, I myself was thinking always in the present.
It was published in *The Metropolitan*

THE CURIOUS CASE OF BENJAMIN BUTTON . Page

This story was inspired by a remark of Mark Twain's to the effect that it was a pity that the best part of life came at the beginning and the worst part at the end. I admit that by trying the experiment upon only one man in a perfectly normal world I have not given his idea a fair trial.
The story was published in Collier's during the summer of 1922.

TARQUIN OF CHEAPSIDE . . . . . . Page

Written almost six years ago, this story is a product of undergraduate days at Princeton. Somewhat revised, it was published in the *Smart Set* in 1921. At the time of its conception I had but one idea—to be a great poet—immediately, and the fact that I was interested in the sound and ring of every phrase, that I dreaded the obvious in prose if not in plot, shows throughout. Probably the peculiar affection I feel for it depends more upon its age than upon any intrinsic merit it may possess. I include it among the fantasies rather because of the treatment than because of the subject.

CONTENTS   vii

AND SO FORTH

THE CRUSTS OF LOVE . . . . Page

Of this story I can say only that it came to me in an irresistible form, crying to be written. It will be accused perhaps of being a mere piece of sentimentality, but, as I saw it, it was a great deal more. If it lacks the ring of sincerity, or even of tragedy, the fault rests not with the theme but with my handling of it.
It appeared in the *Chicago Tribune* and later obtained, I believe, the quadruple gold laurel leaf or some such encomium from one of the many anthologists who at present flourish among us. The gentleman I refer to runs as a rule to stark melodramas with a volcano or the ghost of John Paul Jones in the role of Nemesis, melodramas carefully disguised by early paragraphs in the Jamesian manner which hint dark and subtle complexities to follow. On this order:
"The case of Shaw McPhee, curiously enough, had no bearing on the almost incredible attitude of Martin Sulo. This is parenthetical and, to at least three observers, whose names for the present I must conceal, it seems improbable, etc., etc., etc." until the poor rat of fiction is at last forced out into the open and the melodrama begins.

TWO FOR A CENT . . . . Page

This is my third story of Jelly-Bean Town—or, rather, of Tarleton, Georgia. It is the second story I have written in which no woman is either presented or implied. It appeared in *The Metropolitan* last April.

JEMIMA . . . . Page

We will close on a jovial note. This sketch was published in *Vanity Fair* and for its technique I must apologize to Mr. Stephen Leacock. I have laughed over it a great deal, especially when I first wrote it, but I can laugh over it no longer. Still, as mnay people tell me it is amusing, I include it here. It seems to me worth preserving a few years—at least until the ennui of changing fashions suppresses me, my books, and it together.
With due apologies for this impossible table of contents, I tender these tales of the Jazz Age into the hands of those who read as they run and run as they read.

29

20. Contract with Scribners for *The Great Gatsby*, December 22, 1924.

Scribners was a venerable house that considered publishing to be a gentleman's occupation. Book contracts issued by this publishing company were two pages long and did not treat serial and movie rights, which were worked out as needed. The contract for *The Great Gatsby* gave Fitzgerald 15 percent of the $2.00 price on the first 40,000 copies and 20 percent thereafter. Although the contract does not specify an advance, Scribners routinely granted Fitzgerald loans against his future earnings.

21. *The Great Gatsby* (New York: Scribners, 1925), dust jacket by Francis Cugat.

Francis Cugat's jacket design is more surreal than Edward Hill's realistic portraits for the earlier novels (see item 125). Fitzgerald's comment to Perkins, "For Christs sake don't give anyone that jacket you're saving for me. I've written it into the book" (*Life in Letters*, p. 79), has not been fully explained, but it may refer to Nick Carraway's statement in Chapter IV: "Unlike Gatsby and Tom Buchanan, I had no girl whose disembodied face floated along the dark cornices and blinding signs. . . ."

The Great Gatsby was a commercial failure, selling only about 23,000 copies in 1925, a disappointment that Fitzgerald blamed on its lack of a strong woman character who could appeal to women readers and that Perkins attributed to the reviewers' failure to comprehend the novel fully. See color insert.

22. *The Great Gatsby* **(London: Chatto & Windus, 1926).**

On June 15 Collins, Fitzgerald's English publisher, turned down *Gatsby*, declaring that "to publish 'The Great Gatsby' would be to reduce the number of his readers rather than to increase them" (L. E. Pollinger to Curtis Brown, Scribners Archives). The work was placed the next month with Chatto & Windus, which remained Fitzgerald's English publisher for *Tender Is the Night*. The August 1925 publication consisted of 3,000 copies; the circular red label "2/-" indicates this copy was remaindered and the price reduced from 7/6. See color insert.

---

23. *Tender Is the Night*, *Scribner's Magazine* **(January 1934).**

Tender Is the Night was serialized in *Scribner's Magazine* from January to April 1934. The division into monthly installments may have harmed the novel's reception by obscuring the structure of the novel, and Fitzgerald suspected that some critics read it only in serial form (see item 9).

Edward Shenton's pen-and-ink "decorations" for the serial also appeared in the first edition of the book (see item 136).

24. Maxwell Perkins to Fitzgerald, December 17, 1929, New York City, TLS, 4 pp.

This letter discusses the celebrated boxing match in Paris between Ernest Hemingway and Canadian novelist Morley Callaghan. Although smaller than Hemingway, Callaghan claimed to have knocked Hemingway off his feet. Hemingway blamed his beating on Fitzgerald. Serving as timekeeper, Fitzgerald had become so absorbed in watching the match that he allowed a round to run too long.

When a story claiming Callaghan had knocked out Hemingway appeared in the *New York Herald Tribune* on November 24, 1929, Fitzgerald (at Hemingway's urging) wired Callaghan, insisting that he order a correction to the story. Callaghan, who had already notified the *Tribune* (the correction ran on December 8), reacted angrily to Fitzgerald's cable. Perkins tried to mediate among the three writers, and Fitzgerald and Hemingway did mend the rift in their friendship (*Fitzgerald and Hemingway*, pp. 120–127).

The letter also mentions the planned divorce of Thomas and Peggy Boyd, the latter of whom published under the pen name Woodward Boyd. Fitzgerald had recruited Hemingway and the Boyds for Scribners' fiction list.

CHARLES SCRIBNER'S SONS
PUBLISHERS
FIFTH AVENUE AT 48TH STREET

NEW YORK Dec. 17, 1929

Dear Scott:

I am enclosing a letter I got from Callaghan, and a note which he sent to the Herald Tribune, and which was printed there. They will show you how things stand. The girl who started this story is one Caroline Bancroft. She wanders around Europe every year and picks up what she can in the way of gossip, and prints it in the Denver paper, and it spreads from there. Callaghan told me the whole story about boxing with Ernest, and the point he put the most emphasis on was your time-keeping. That impressed him a great deal. He did say that he knew he was more adept in boxing than Ernest, and that he had been practising for several years with fighters. He was all right about the whole matter. He is much better than he looks.

As for Tom Boyd, he is in Reno where that Mrs. Bartlett is getting a divorce. This takes until January, and if Peggy goes ahead with her side of the divorce matter and gets Tom free, those two will be married and apparently plan to live in Woodstock, Vermont. All reports indicate that Tom is satisfied, but I think he has got himself badly hooked. He got into some kind of a fight out in Reno during a party, and was arrested and fined, and I guess he feels pretty badly about that. The story that appeared in the News was awful, but I suppose the fact was that he wanted to kill some man, as it seems he generally does when he

25. Maxwell Perkins to Fitzgerald, April 8, 1938, New York City, TLS, 4 pp.

Perkins relates Hemingway's recent departure to report on the Spanish Civil War and the merits of Hemingway's new play, *The Fifth Column*. Taken with Perkins's letter of December 17, 1929, this letter attests to Perkins's determination to foster good relations among his sometimes fractious writers and to encourage them to continue to solidify their literary connections (see items 24 and 72).

26. *Tender Is the Night* (New York: Scribners, 1934), review copy bound in wrappers made from the dust jacket.

Fitzgerald had high hopes for the commercial success of this tale of the deterioration of American doctor Richard Diver under the influence of the idle wealthy in Europe.

Concerned that Fitzgerald's celebrity as a short-story writer had eclipsed his reputation as a novelist, Scribners pushed hard for the success of *Tender*. The novel's critical reception suffered when some reviewers found the portrayal of Diver's decline unconvincing, probably because of the insufficient number of clear and consistent time signals in the novel. See color insert.

27. *Tender Is the Night* (New York: Scribners, 1934).

The first printing of 7,600 copies of *Tender Is the Night*, published April 12, 1934, sold quickly. Scribners followed up this success with a printing of 5,075 and one of 2,520, both within a six-week period. The novel placed tenth on the *Publishers' Weekly* best-seller lists for April and May, but the $5,104.65 in royalties were not enough to pay off Fitzgerald's debts to Scribners. See color insert.

"The Metamorphosis of Amateur into Professional"
Entering Short-Story Markets

by Tracy Simmons Bitonti

F. Scott Fitzgerald's magazine work is an integral aspect of his career as a professional author. His stories, which were written for money and with thought to audience tastes, provided a sustained means of income. They are also important because of their close thematic and stylistic relationships to his novels—Fitzgerald used his stories as workshops in which to test material and develop ideas. He labored diligently on them for their magazine appearances and revised them for his story collections, disproving the notion that he was frivolous with his talent or that his writing came easily.

As a short-story writer, Fitzgerald was, in his time, primarily associated with *The Saturday Evening Post*, though only 40 percent of his more than 160 stories appeared in that publication. Several other magazines served different but equally important functions in his development. At the beginning of his career he tested various magazine venues, and after he was no longer able to satisfy *Post* requirements, he found a new market in *Esquire*. Fitzgerald's relationships with these different magazines provide essential insights into his achievement.

Fitzgerald served a literary apprenticeship writing for the publications of the schools he attended, including the *Nassau Literary Magazine* at Princeton. The first story for which he was paid was "Babes in the Woods," a revised *Nassau Lit* story that was published in the September 1919 issue of *The Smart Set*. Though its circulation at the time was relatively small at 22,000, *The Smart Set* was a highly regarded magazine with a sophisticated image. Its editors were George Jean Nathan, a respected drama critic, and H. L. Mencken, the most influential social and literary critic in America. The magazine soon published more Fitzgerald material, including "Porcelain and Pink," a short play, in the January 1920 issue, and the stories "Benediction" and "Dalyrimple Goes Wrong," both in the February 1920 issue. This exposure, in conjunction with his first *Saturday Evening Post* publication ("Head and Shoulders" in February 1920), served to promote the author of *This Side of Paradise* to the different readerships of those magazines.

The Smart Set and *The American Mercury*, the influential *Smart Set* successor Mencken edited from 1924 to 1933, published stories that were not salable to more-popular magazines such as the *Post*, for reasons of length or subject. *The Smart Set* printed two major stories: "May Day" (July 1920) and "The Diamond as Big as the Ritz" (June 1922); and *The American Mercury* published "Absolution" (June 1924) and "Crazy Sunday" (October 1932). Fitzgerald had written "Diamond" and "Crazy Sunday" with the *Post* in mind, but when the *Post* and other popular magazines declined them, he turned to Mencken's publications. These magazines were much lower on the pay scale ("Crazy Sunday" brought $200 in a year in which Fitzgerald was getting $4,000 from the *Post*) but were more responsive to Fitzgerald's serious themes (such as the negative effects of wealth on character in "Diamond"). The popular magazines tended to avoid such subjects, as Fitzgerald discovered when "Diamond" was rejected by the *Post* and *Harper's Bazaar* and when "Crazy Sunday" was turned down by the "slicks" to which it was offered. While his lesser work appeared in the commercial publications, not all of Fitzgerald's quality stories went to the elite periodicals: the "slicks" published such noteworthy efforts as "Winter Dreams" (*Metropolitan*, December 1922), and the *Smart Set* printed such minor pieces as "Tarquin of Cheapside" (February 1921; previously published in the *Nassau Lit*).

Another magazine significant to Fitzgerald's career was *Scribner's Magazine*, parented by the publisher of his novels. He placed only two stories there—"The Cut-

Glass Bowl" (May 1920) and "The Four Fists" (June 1920)—but the magazine was strategically important in publicizing the newly released *This Side of Paradise*. Not only did the stories expose him to another set of readers—an educated, genteel audience—but the reputable magazine also touted Scribners' new author on the "Book Notes" pages of those issues. Fitzgerald was learning how to shape his material for particular audiences: the didacticism of these two stories (their main weakness) made them appropriate for the conservative *Scribner's*. Fitzgerald explained to Princeton University president John Grier Hibben that "The Four Fists" was written "in desperation one evening because I had a three inch pile of rejection slips and it was financially nessesary for me to give the magazines what they wanted" (*Life in Letters*, p. 40). But he did not, as Hemingway asserted, deliberately "ruin" his stories by altering finished drafts just to make them salable. For example, when he sent "The Jelly Bean" to his agent, Harold Ober, in June 1920, he was firm in his intent: "I've shortened this story a little and what's more I think I've managed to improve it—but I think it'd spoil it utterly to give it a happy ending" (*As Ever, Scott Fitz—*, p. 15).

After at first experimenting with a variety of magazines, Fitzgerald settled into an almost-exclusive relationship with the *Post*. But as events in his life began to wear him down in the mid-1930s, he lost the ability to write *Post* stories. He formed an affiliation with *Esquire*, a sophisticated new men's magazine featuring fiction, articles, sports, humor, fashion, art, and cartoons. Its founding editor, Arnold Gingrich, was able to attract many of the nation's best authors, including Ernest Hemingway, John Dos Passos, Irwin Shaw, and Langston Hughes, to write for the magazine. Its circulation was about 130,000 in its early years and was more than 468,000 when Fitzgerald died in 1940. He began writing for *Esquire* in 1934, and from 1936 until his death almost all of his work was published there. Though at $250–300 per story it was on the low end of the pay scale, *Esquire* provided Fitzgerald with a vital source of income, particularly important after his M-G-M contract ended in January 1939. The money he earned from *Esquire* stories helped to buy Fitzgerald some time to work on his novel, *The Love of the Last Tycoon*. Fitzgerald had used his story writing to finance his novel writing before; but this time he was not using the stories as a workshop as he had previously. His stories of this period did not include material worth recycling.

Esquire is also significant in Fitzgerald's career because it was in this forum that he published the "Crack-Up" essays and other autobiographical reflections, casting himself in a different light from his 1920s image. The essays are generally better than the *Esquire* stories. The "Crack-Up" series, which was written specifically for *Esquire*, generated a substantial and largely negative reaction among Fitzgerald's readers and contemporaries, but the response proves that Fitzgerald was still being read by magazine audiences in 1936.

The *Esquire* stories mark a shift in Fitzgerald's literary style, as he began working more frequently in the form of the "short-short story": compressed, economical sketches of 1,000–2,000 words, very different from his sometimes over-plotted *Post* stories of 4,000–6,000 words. Some of the stories written in this period were rejected by other magazines first, and Fitzgerald regretted the economic necessity of sending them to *Esquire*. Most, however, were written with *Esquire* in mind, and the low pay and Gingrich's relative leniency in what he would accept undoubtedly contributed to Fitzgerald's use of the shorter form.

In an essay titled "Early Success," first published in *American Cavalcade* in October 1937 and collected in *The Crack-Up*, Fitzgerald described the process that occurred while he waited for the publication of his first novel:

> . . . the metamorphosis of amateur into professional began to take place—a sort of stitching together of your whole life into a pattern of work, so that the end of one job is automatically the beginning of another. (*Crack-Up*, p. 86)

His exploration of short-story markets was a significant part of that process.

◆ ◆ ◆

28. Fitzgerald to Lorena and Philip McQuillan, December 28, 1920, New York City, ALS, 3 pp.

In this letter to his aunt and uncle, Fitzgerald expresses his determination to be "a sincere writer." He makes the distinction between artistic integrity and popular success, a fine line he would walk for the rest of his career. He also indicates his awareness of the expectations of the magazine marketplace, understanding that it was not the best outlet for his "pessimistic" writing. The letter continues: "I have a contract you know with the Metropolitan Magazine to serialize my next novel for $7000 but I'm sure if they tried to do this one their circulation would drop. You know the stuff they want!" The novel he refers to was most likely an early version of *The Beautiful and Damned* (see item 17). The letter also offers evidence of the influence of critic and *Smart Set* editor H. L. Mencken: Fitzgerald refers to him as "my current idol." Mencken's championing of realism and naturalism had encouraged Fitzgerald to write in the "pessimistic" vein of *The Beautiful and Damned*.

29. "The Four Fists," *Scribner's Magazine* (June 1920).

Scribner's drew extra attention to "The Four Fists" by making it one of the issue's illustrated features. In addition the "Book Notes" section indicates that *This Side of Paradise* had reached its third "edition" three weeks after its publication and that Fitzgerald was "already known for a highly popular series of stories which have been appearing in the *Saturday Evening Post*."

30. H. L. Mencken, *Prejudices: Second Series* (New York: Knopf, 1920), inscribed to Fitzgerald on free front endpaper.

The inscription is evidence of the friendship between the two men. This volume also shows further proof of Mencken's influence: Fitzgerald underlined and annotated passages in the section of the book titled "The National Letters," in which Mencken discusses the continued lack of a great American literary tradition. Fitzgerald also reviewed the book for the March 1921 issue of *Bookman*.

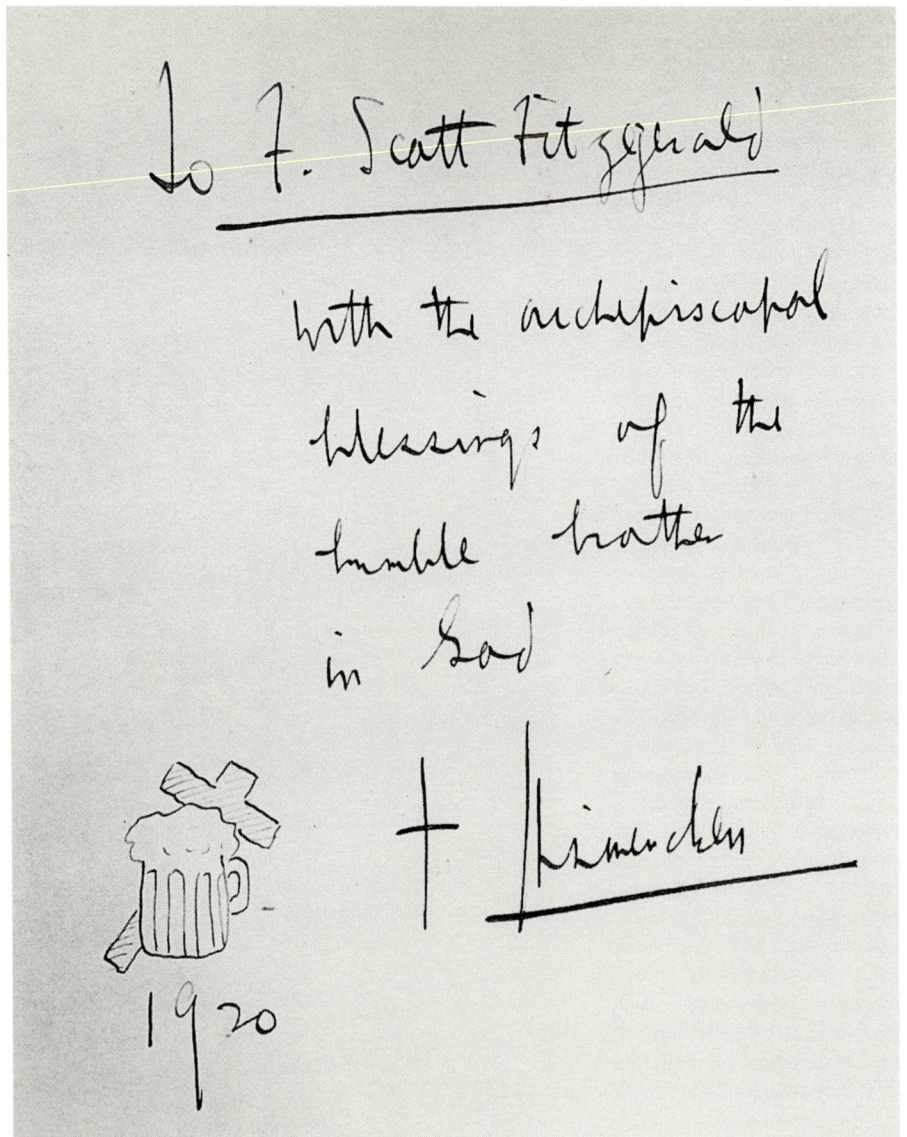

31. "May Day," *The Smart Set* (July 1920); *Tales of the Jazz Age* (New York: Scribners, 1922).

Fitzgerald's long story "May Day" appeared first in *The Smart Set* and was republished in *Tales of the Jazz Age*. Whenever one of his stories was reprinted, Fitzgerald would revise it—partly because he was dedicated to honing his craft and partly because he often lifted his own story material for use in his novels; he scrupulously avoided repeating himself in his books. Fitzgerald made revisions throughout "May Day" to tighten his prose and to improve character depiction; but the most significant alteration is the ending. In the book version Gordon Sterrett's suicide is presented directly. In this case Fitzgerald revised not because he had reused the material but because he saw that the action could be clarified.

32. "The Couple," RTS and MS, 37 pp.

This story was probably written between 1920 and 1924, but it was never published, nor is there evidence that it was offered to magazines. The first twenty-four pages are typed, double-spaced, with Fitzgerald's pencil revisions; the remaining thirteen pages are manuscript. The story depicts a young couple, Carrol and Lou Pawling, who are separating after a year of marriage but who have agreed to stay in the same house for a final two weeks until arrangements can be made. Carrol has hired a husband-and-wife team of servants, Reynolds and Katy, who prove to be ridiculously inept and, when dismissed, belligerent. Arguing in their defense, Katy reveals to Pawling that Carrol has been miserable about her impending divorce from him; the revelation sparks a reconciliation. Fitzgerald's markings and changes on these pages indicate his careful attention to his writing. But the story is not up to Fitzgerald's usual standards—the servants' behavior is implausible. The plot is the kind of light entertainment a magazine such as the *Post* would have wanted, but Fitzgerald apparently lost interest. As he would write to Zelda Fitzgerald in 1940, "As soon as I feel I am writing to a cheap specification my pen freezes and my talent vanishes over the hill" (*Life in Letters*, p. 444).

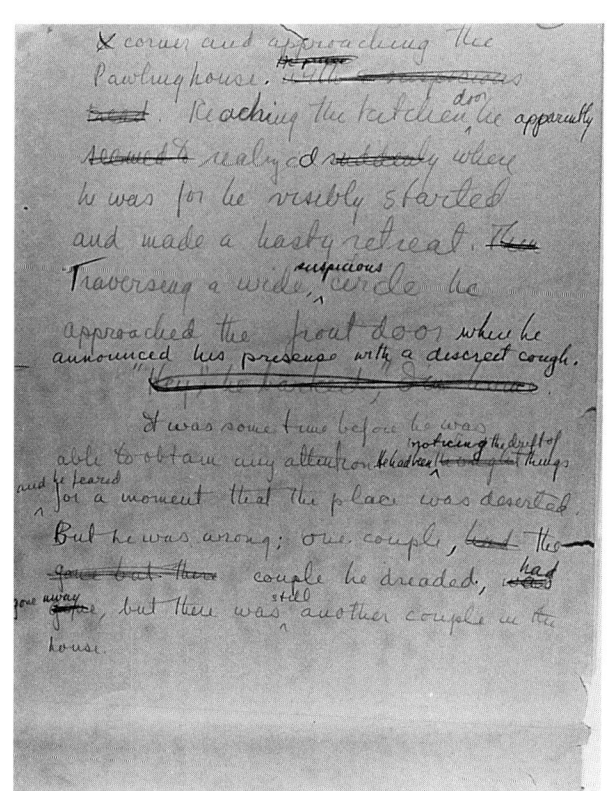

33. *This Side of Paradise* (London: Collins, 1921), inscribed to F. R. Henderson on free front endpaper, with newspaper clipping and mimeographed blurbs from Sinclair Lewis and H. L. Mencken glued onto front endpapers.

It is not known who Henderson was or who pasted in the clippings, but the note under the newspaper photograph is in Fitzgerald's hand. The Fitzgeralds were on their first trip to Europe in 1921, and their visit to England coincided with the first British publication of *This Side of Paradise* (on May 26). Fitzgerald had been anticipating an enthusiastic reaction similar to the American reception and was disappointed by the lukewarm response.

Fitzgerald used his short stories as workshops for his novels, testing themes and "recycling" passages or phrases he liked. *This Side of Paradise* incorporates revised versions of "Babes in the Woods" and "The Debutante," both of which had previously appeared in the *Nassau Literary Magazine* at Princeton and in *The Smart Set*. The workshop process was especially utilized with *The Great Gatsby* and *Tender Is the Night*, each novel having "clusters" of related stories—though none of those stories was incorporated in its entirety as "Babes" and "The Debutante" were.

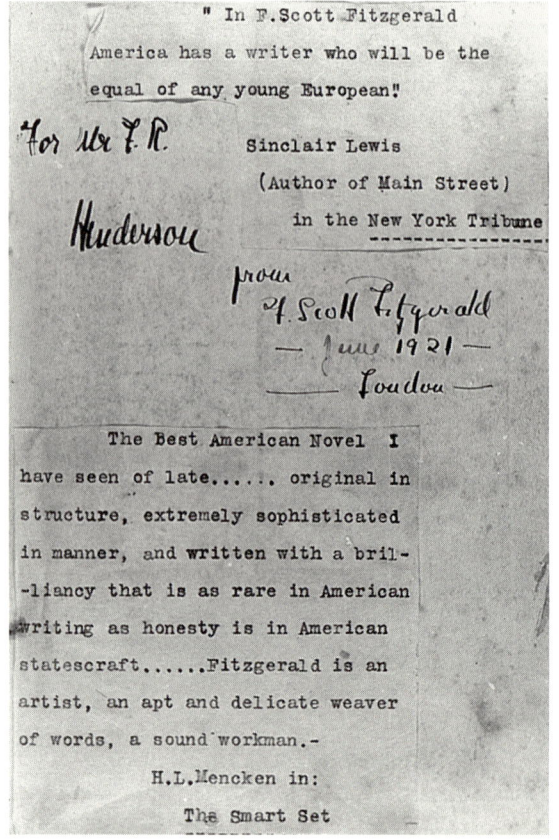

34. Fitzgerald's holograph monthly expenditures for 1923, 1 p.

Fitzgerald kept careful track of his earnings, but he was not always attentive to where the money went. His total income for 1923—from stories and other writings, movie rights, advances on *The Vegetable* and *The Great Gatsby*, and book royalties—was $28,759.78. With allocations such as $100 for "Wild Parties" and large "miscelaeneous" sums, the Fitzgeralds were not living within their means—and there was also the matter of the faintly noted "MISSING $1000.00" per month beyond that. Such spending habits and later school and medical expenses meant that Fitzgerald needed top prices for his writing; and the stories earned much more than the novels. Fitzgerald turned his 1923 budget woes into a humorous essay titled "How to Live on $36,000 a Year," which appeared in the *Post* on April 5, 1924, and for which he was paid $1,000 (less Harold Ober's 10 percent commission).

Monthly Expenditure 1923			
TAXES	200.00	**TRIPS, PLEASURE + PARTIES**	
RENT	300.00		
FOOD	200.00	House Liquor	80.00 (apportioned per 1 year)
COAL + WOOD	35.00	PLAZA	26.50
ICE	8.50	ALABAMA	33.00
GAS	27.00	ATLANTIC CITY	10.00
LIGHT	14.50	THEATRE	20.00
PHONE	25.00	BARBER	10.00
WATER	5.00	HAIR DRESSING	15.00
		CHARITY	4.00
SERVANTS	295.00	WILD PARTIES	100.00
		Taxis	15.00
DOCTORS	42.50	Gambling	33.00
DRUG STORE	32.50	LUNCHES (N.Y)	25.00
CLUB	105.50	SUBWAY (ect)	29.00
		Miscelaeneous Cash	276.00
NEWSPAPERS	5.00		
BOOKS	14.50	MISS 1$	
FLOWERS	9.00		
AUTO	23.00		
PLUMBER	13.50		
ELECTRIC	1.50		
COMMUTATION	4.00		
SCOTT'S CLOTHES	33.00		
ZELDA'S CLOTHES	100.00		
BABY'S CLOTHES	25.00		
HOUSEHOLD AND MISCELLANEOUS CHARGES	81.00		785.60
			1690.40
TYPING	12.00		2396.00
	1620.40		

35. "The Diamond as Big as the Ritz," *The Smart Set* (June 1922).

The cover art for this issue (see color insert) has nothing to do with Fitzgerald's story, but it reflects the magazine's sophisticated image. Fitzgerald had initially hoped that the story would sell to a higher-paying magazine, but he was learning enough about the marketplace to realize that its length and subject would be problematic for the "slicks." On February 5, 1922, he wrote Ober:

> In short I realize I *can't* get a real good price for the three weeks work that story represents—so I'd much rather get no price but reap the subtle, and nowadays oh-so-valuable dividend that comes from Mencken's good graces. Besides, in the *Smart Set* it will be featured. (*Life in Letters*, p. 54)

Fitzgerald was paid $300 for the story.

36. *The Vegetable* (New York: Scribners, 1923), inscribed to Harold and Anne Ober on free front endpaper.

Fitzgerald's first story sales to the *Smart Set* and *Scribner's Magazine* were made on his own. In October 1919 he began sending his material to the Paul Revere Reynolds literary agency and soon became the client of Harold Ober, who successfully marketed the stories. Ober provided Fitzgerald with guidance as to the expectations of the marketplace; even more important, he, like Maxwell Perkins, provided Fitzgerald with emergency personal loans. The inscription in this copy of Fitzgerald's play reflects the reserved nature of their relationship. See color insert.

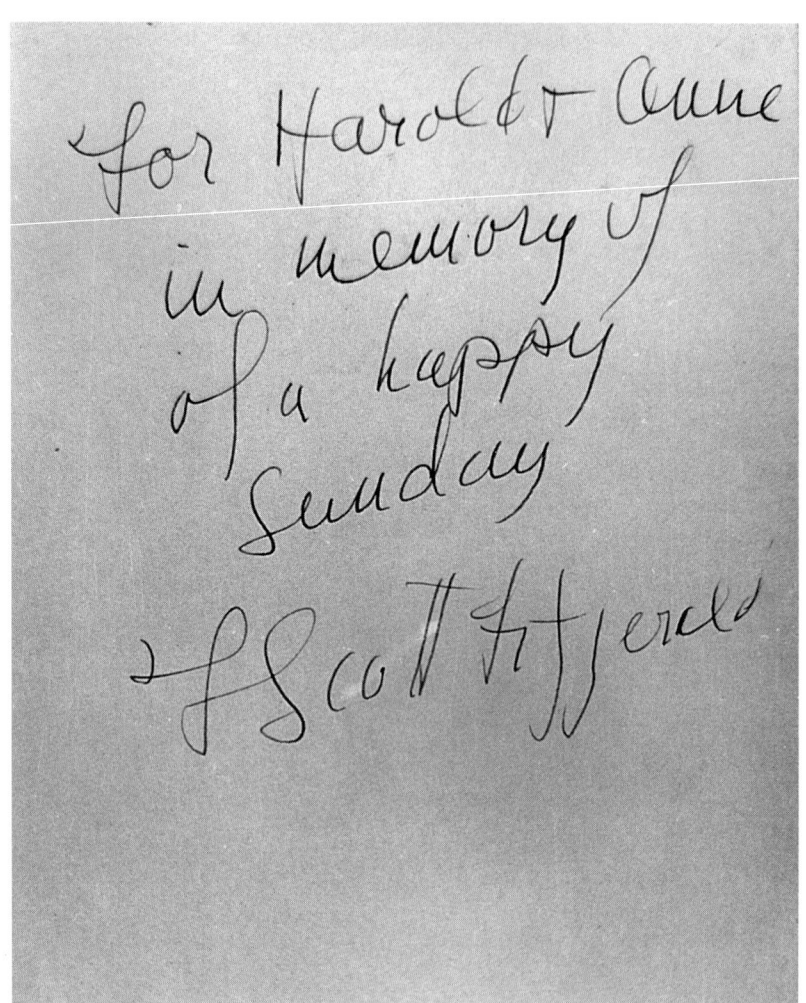

37. "Outside the Cabinet-Maker's," *The Century Magazine* (December 1928).

"Outside the Cabinet-Maker's" is an anomaly in Fitzgerald's story canon. This brief depiction of the conversation of a man and his six-year-old daughter was rejected by several magazines and ultimately brought Fitzgerald $150 in a year during which he was making $3,500 from *Post* stories. It is the only extant example of Fitzgerald's writing in the "short-short story" form before the appearance of his *Esquire* pieces. The story portrays the father's attempt to share his daughter's world and to express his devotion.

38. Fitzgerald to Scottie Fitzgerald, January 1928, Canada, postcards.

The connection of "Outside the Cabinet-Maker's" to Fitzgerald's love for his own daughter, Scottie, is seen in a series of postcards he wrote to her from Canada. He sketched on the fronts ("the man with three noses" is a recurring character) and wrote teasing, humorous messages on the backs. On the second one shown, he foreshadows a bit of dialogue in the story as he suggests the daughter's nonchalant confidence in her father's affection (see color insert and items 181–183).

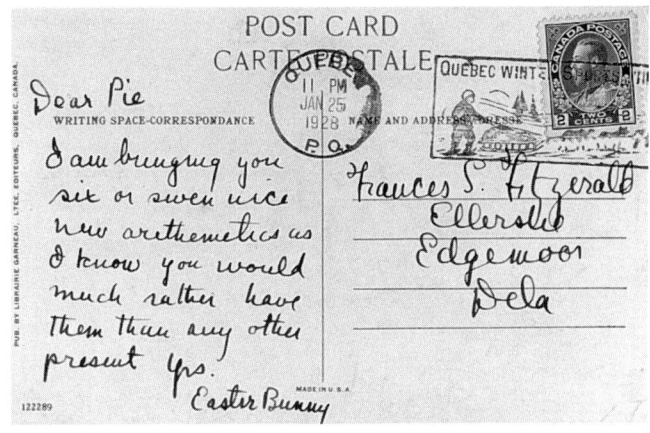

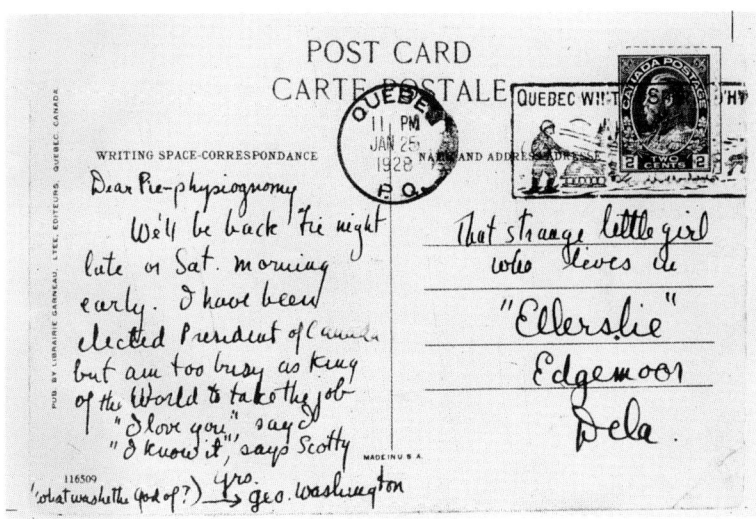

39. Page from *F. Scott Fitzgerald's Ledger* (Washington: Bruccoli Clark/NCR Microcard Books, 1973) indicating his earnings for 1929.

The *Ledger*, a document that Fitzgerald maintained from about 1920 to about 1937, includes records of his earnings and of everything he wrote, indicating where each work had been published and whether he had "stripped" it (cutting out the best parts for further use in his novels), as well as his "Outline Chart of My Life." The record for 1929 shows clearly the disparity between the amount of money his book royalties brought ($31.77 for eight titles including the British edition of *The Great Gatsby*) and the amount he made from his magazine writing ($27,000). Fitzgerald did not maintain his *Ledger* after 1937, during the years in Hollywood when he was making only $250–300 per story from *Esquire*.

40. "Crazy Sunday," *The American Mercury* **(October 1932).**

This Hollywood story was rejected by the *Post* and other "slick" magazines before Mencken accepted it. Ober explained in a February 1932 letter to Fitzgerald that the *Post* and the women's magazines were put off by the dubious moral situation at the end: as Ober describes it, "A wife who has just heard that her husband has been killed wants another man to stay with her." Also, the Hearst publications "wouldn't dare to use the story as they were afraid it might offend the moving picture people with whom they are affiliated" (*As Ever, Scott Fitz—*, p. 189).

41. Contract with Scribners for publication of "A New Collection of Short Stories," June 12, 1934.

As this contract for the then-untitled *Taps at Reveille* (New York: Scribners, 1935) indicates, Fitzgerald—despite the fact that volumes of short stories generally do not sell as well as novels—received the same royalty rate for all books: 15 percent of the retail price for the first 20,000 copies sold; 17.5 percent for the next 20,000; and 20 percent for all copies sold beyond 40,000. None of the collections reached the first 20,000 copies; *Taps* did not sell beyond its first printing of 5,100 copies.

Fitzgerald put a great deal of work into his story collections, deciding which stories to include and making suggestions for how to design and market the volumes. Fitzgerald believed that the magazine appearances of his stories were ephemeral but that the ones collected in book form would have permanence and affect his critical reputation. He tried to show a representative variety of his talents; for example, sending "The Night before Chancellorsville" to Perkins for inclusion in *Taps*, he wrote: "My idea is that this and 'The Fiend' [both *Esquire* sketches] would give people less chance to say they are all standardized *Saturday Evening Post* stories" (*Dear Scott/Dear Max*, p. 215). He also revised carefully, both to improve the stories and to expunge passages he had used in his novels. He felt strongly about this issue, as he wrote to Perkins: ". . . I can't think of anything that would more annoy or disillusion a reader than to find an author using a phrase over and over as if his imagination were starving" (*Dear Scott/Dear Max*, p. 215). Fitzgerald's story collections were not primarily intended to cash in on work he had already done.

42. Fitzgerald to Harold and Anne Ober, n.d. [December 25, 1937], Hollywood, Calif., telegram: MERRY CHRISTMAS TO TWO PEOPLE WHO MADE AN OLD YEAR POSSIBLE AND A NEW YEAR HAPPY= SCOTT FITZGERALD.

Fitzgerald's message to the Obers reflects their economic importance to him. Fitzgerald was spending his first Christmas in Hollywood, where he was working as a screenwriter. At the time he went to Hollywood, he owed Ober more than $12,000—a debt he repaid. In 1939, when Ober discontinued his custom of sending Fitzgerald advances on story sales, their business relationship dissolved.

43. "Financing Finnegan," *Esquire* **(January 1938).**

Esquire became Fitzgerald's primary venue during the last two years of his life. His name was usually first in the list of contributors under "Fiction" or "Articles" on the cover, thus indicating either his continuing popularity among magazine readers or editor Arnold Gingrich's regard for him. "Financing Finnegan" is a private joke in which Fitzgerald wryly depicts a writer's living on loans from his editor and agent. When Fitzgerald wrote the story in June 1937, he had hoped the *Post* would take it. But editors at the magazine declined, calling the story "amusing" but saying it would not "interest a wide market"; and by August 3 Fitzgerald had to send a postcard to Ober: "Better Send *Finnegan* to Esquire as if it came Straight from me. I already owe them for it" (*As Ever, Scott Fitz—*, pp. 320, 334). It was the only fiction Fitzgerald published that year.

44. Fitzgerald to Scottie Fitzgerald, September 21 [1939], Encino, Calif., telegram.

This message to his daughter emphasizes the direct economic importance of Fitzgerald's magazine writing and specifies *Esquire* as an essential source of money during the last years of his life. In this case he borrowed from *Esquire* (against his story sales) to pay Scottie Fitzgerald's Vassar College tuition. He wanted his daughter to be able to attend a good college and his wife to have the best psychiatric care; these bills made it necessary for him to keep generating sufficient funds.

45. H. L. Mencken to an unidentified bookseller, June 17, 1946, Baltimore, Md., TLS, 1 p.—framed with photograph of Mencken.

Mencken's continued interest in Fitzgerald's work is shown by this order for a copy of *The Crack-Up*, which had been published in 1945. The volume (which includes the "Crack-Up" series and seven other autobiographical essays, letters, and portions of Fitzgerald's notebooks) was widely read and has never gone out of print, contributing to the "Fitzgerald revival."

"Each Time in a New Disguise"
The Author as a Commercial Magazinist

by Park Bucker

On February 21, 1920, F. Scott Fitzgerald entered the commercial magazine marketplace when *The Saturday Evening Post* published "Head and Shoulders," a bittersweet comedy of young love. With a circulation of more than 2,750,000 weekly readers and a cost of one nickel, the *Post* offered writers the highest prices and the widest outlet for popular fiction in America. By the end of May 1920 the *Post* published five more stories by Fitzgerald, placing them prominently and listing his name on the magazine's cover. That spring his first novel, *This Side of Paradise,* appeared to critical praise, and he married Zelda Sayre after a tumultuous courtship. All before he was twenty-four years old.

Within the space of a few months the young author had experienced financial, romantic, artistic, and popular success; he had achieved the happy ending. Thirteen years after this early triumph, Fitzgerald maintained in "One Hundred False Starts" that all authors repeat themselves: "We have two or three great and moving experiences in our lives . . . and we tell our two or three stories—each time in a new disguise—maybe ten times, maybe a hundred, as long as people will listen" (*Afternoon of an Author,* p. 132).

Fitzgerald's experience of youthful success permeates his best commercial fiction, ranging from the exuberance of his early romantic comedies to the regretful recollections and wasted opportunities of his later stories. Whereas much of this period's commercial fiction reads as mawkish and overly sentimental, Fitzgerald's happy endings and bittersweet romances transcend the genre because they spring from his personal experience. Despite unlikely plots and contrived situations, Fitzgerald's stories combine well-written prose with sincere emotional content.

Fitzgerald placed more than 130 of his 160-odd published stories in glossy, mass-circulation magazines, commonly known as "slicks." For seventeen years these stories, Fitzgerald's chief source of income, generated much more revenue than he received from his novels. He earned $400 for his first *Post* appearance, but in less than ten years his commercial price rose to $4,000 per story.

The large popular-fiction marketplace enjoyed by the reading public of the 1920s and 1930s has essentially vanished today. Before the age of television, magazine fiction represented a major source of popular entertainment on a national scale. Heavily illustrated, the slicks offered humor, melodrama, information, and escape to millions of readers. In accordance with popular tastes they also appealed to social and political conservatism.

Yet Fitzgerald, a social realist, enjoyed much success in this constraining forum. Despite the bathtub-gin-and-flapper image associated with him, Fitzgerald's short fiction often presented the traditional American theme of an individual's succeeding through intelligence, imagination, determination, and luck. His heroes did not challenge the traditional social structure but rather worked imaginatively within it. They genuinely believed in the American dream of success. In his later stories Fitzgerald examined the tragic aspects of success in which his heroes fail due to dissipation and irresponsible behavior.

For all their craftsmanship and entertainment value, or perhaps because of it, Fitzgerald's commercial stories are still regarded by many critics as mere diversions for the masses: frothy, insubstantial, and unworthy of any close literary attention. Fitzgerald himself fostered this image by deprecating his own commercial achievement to other writers. He wrote Ernest Hemingway in 1929, "the *Post* now pay the old whore $4000. a screw. But now it's because she's mastered the 40 positions—in her youth one was enough" (*Life in Letters*, p. 169).

But in a 1935 letter to his literary agent Harold

Ober, he described the effort and talent that he had to generate to produce commercial fiction: "all my stories are concieved like novels, require a special emotion, a special experience—so that my readers, if such there be, know that each time it will be something new, not in form but in substance (it'd be far better for me if I could do pattern stories but the pencil just goes dead on me)" (*Life in Letters,* p. 284). Although the sale of short stories financed the writing of his novels, Fitzgerald believed that writing commercial fiction depleted his creative reserve.

After his initial exposure in the *Post,* coupled with the success of his first novel, Fitzgerald rapidly became a valuable commodity in the magazine marketplace. Periodicals competed to lure the author away from the *Post. Metropolitan Magazine* optioned his stories for $900 each, a $400 raise from his 1920 *Post* price. When *Metropolitan* went into receivership, the Hearst Corporation optioned his output, paying him $1,500 as a signing bonus.

Because Fitzgerald's stories emphasized youthful concerns and characters, many readers regarded him as the spokesman for his generation. His fiction changed the conventional depiction of young people as naive or innocent, featuring them instead as witty, romantic heroes. He also challenged traditional standards by celebrating beautiful, intelligent, independent, and determined young women in their quest to secure successful marriages.

Following the financial disappointment of *The Great Gatsby* and the end of his Hearst contract, Fitzgerald returned to the *Post* as the steady market for his stories. Between 1926 and 1937, his most productive period as a magazine writer, the *Post* published fifty-two stories by Fitzgerald.

As he experienced many delays in the completion of his fourth novel, Fitzgerald became one of the magazine's most popular and highly paid authors. The author nostalgically recalled his own adolescence in two successful series featuring the recurring characters Basil Duke Lee and Josephine Perry. In accordance with magazine conventions, most of Fitzgerald's *Post* stories end happily, and nearly all contain some representation of romantic love.

Yet personal crises of the early 1930s, coinciding with the economic crash, introduced a somber tone into Fitzgerald's magazine fiction. In such major stories as "One Trip Abroad" (October 11, 1930) and "Babylon Revisited" (February 21, 1931), Fitzgerald explored both the tragic aspects of his own experiences and the reckless behavior of his generation.

In 1932 Fitzgerald's *Post* price dropped from $4,000 to $2,500. Although the decrease may have resulted from falling revenues caused by the Depression, *Post* editors also complained to Ober that Fitzgerald's most recent stories had not been up to his standard. With his magazine fortunes waning, Fitzgerald placed great financial hope in the success of his long-delayed novel, *Tender Is the Night,* finally published in 1934. The novel proved a financial failure, compelling Fitzgerald to return immediately to commercial writing without a respite to renew his creative powers. He made several unsuccessful attempts to generate another magazine series that could provide financial stability through the promised sale of future stories. These efforts failed because Fitzgerald could no longer draw on his own experiences for material, turning instead to artificial sources. In the mid-1930s Fitzgerald's life contained little that would appeal to a commercial market.

On March 6, 1937, Fitzgerald essentially ended his career as a popular fiction writer when the *Post* published "'Trouble,'" his last story to appear in the weekly magazine. The story featured a nurse named "Trouble" and represented Fitzgerald's final attempt to create a popular series character. The *Post* paid $2,000 for the story, placing it third out of the four stories in the issue.

Although Fitzgerald's commercial stories proceed from the same genius that created his novels, they share characteristics that set them apart from his "serious" fiction. The stories display an expansive use of wit and romantic love, and an unashamed celebration of youthful success. After more than fifty years they retain their power to charm, amuse, and move readers.

Two months before his death, Fitzgerald reflected on the end of his career as a commercial magazinist in a letter to his wife, Zelda:

> It's odd that my old talent for the short story vanished. It was partly that times changed, editors changed, but part of it was tied up somehow with you and me—the happy ending. Of course every third story had some other ending but essentially I got my public with stories of young love. I must have had a powerful imagination to project it so far and so often into the past (*Life in Letters,* pp. 467, 469).

46. "Head and Shoulders," *The Saturday Evening Post* (February 21, 1920).

Fitzgerald wrote this story after the sale of his first novel, *This Side of Paradise*, to Scribners. The *Post* printed it one month before the publication of his novel, marking Fitzgerald's first appearance before a mass audience. The magazine paid $400 for the story. Fitzgerald also reached silent-movie audiences with this story when he sold the film rights for $2,500 to Metro Pictures Corporation. Retitled *The Chorus Girl's Romance*, the film starred Viola Dana. The film's lobby card reflected the story's slightly scandalous tone with the description "She shook a wicked shoulder and she owned a wicked wink" (*Romantic Egoists*, p. 74).

Six years after the sale of this story Fitzgerald reminisced to his literary agent Harold Ober about the joy he felt on his first *Post* sale: "I was twenty-two when I came to New York and found that you'd sold *Head and Shoulders* to the Post. I'd like to get a thrill like that again but I suppose its only once in a lifetime" (*Life in Letters*, p. 93).

47. Fitzgerald to Isabelle Amorous, February 29, 1920, Princeton, N.J., ALS, 2 pp.

Isabelle Amorous was the sister of Fitzgerald's Newman School–friend Martin. In this letter he boasts about his recent magazine success and responds to Isabelle's concern over the resumption of his engagement with Zelda Sayre. Fitzgerald asserts later in the letter that he "fell in love with her courage, her sincerity and her flaming self respect and its these things I'd believe in even if the whole world indulged in wild suspicions that she wasn't all that she should be." Zelda agreed to marry him after Scribners accepted *This Side of Paradise*. The letter was written before the novel's publication in March 1920. With the proceeds from the movie sale of *Head and Shoulders* Fitzgerald bought his fiancee a platinum-and-diamond wristwatch.

48. Fitzgerald to Robert D. Clark, February 9, 1921, New York City, ALS, 4 pp.

In 1921 Fitzgerald was regarded as the spokesman for the rebellious younger generation. In this letter Fitzgerald responds to criticism from his boyhood friend Robert D. Clark and defends his recent popular success. He rejects conventional "real people" and traditional tenets, allying himself instead with innovative writers such as Shelley, Whitman, Poe, Swinburne, and Shaw. Fitzgerald identifies himself with Shakespeare by inserting a mock letter from "Mrs. Shakespeare" in which she criticizes her son's controversial success.

Throughout his career Fitzgerald felt compelled to justify his role as a popular commercial writer. In 1930 he defended his magazine fiction to Ober with "These *Post* stories *in* the *Post* are at least not any spot on me—they're honest and if they're *form* is stereotyped people know what to *expect when* they pick up the *Post*" (*Life in Letters*, p. 183). In a 1932 letter to his wife's psychiatrist, Fitzgerald described his commercial stories as "sections, debased, over-simplified, if you like, of my own soul" (*Life in Letters*, p. 221).

49. "The Offshore Pirate," RTS, 1 p.; "The Offshore Pirate," *The Saturday Evening Post* (May 29, 1920); *Flappers and Philosophers* (New York: Scribners, 1920).

The page presents the original ending for Fitzgerald's sixth *Post* story. Initially titled "The Proud Piracy," the story portrays the hijacking of a yacht with a beautiful and imperious young woman aboard. Fitzgerald originally ended the fanciful story as nothing more than Ardita's dream of a gentleman pirate. In the story's final version Fitzgerald transformed a weak conclusion into one of wit and imagination. Instead of consigning the entire adventure to the heroine's dream, Fitzgerald maintains the fantasy to the last sentence of the story: "reaching up on her tiptoes she kissed him softly in the illustration" (*F&P*, p. 46). This final image underscores the story's theme of theatricality and imaginative artifice.

Fitzgerald wrote his literary agent that "The last line takes Mr. Lorimer [editor of the *Post*] at his word. Its one of the best lines I've ever written" (*As Ever, Scott Fitz—*, p. 12). But the *Post* omitted the final line, perhaps because no corresponding illustration appeared next to that particular text in the magazine. The story was published with Fitzgerald's revised ending when it appeared in *Flappers and Philosophers*, which does not include illustrations.

... Ardita's eyes opened slowly. It was very dark and quiet and she realized that it must be quite late. Her book had fallen from her

(38)

lap, but in her hand she still clutched the remains of a sucked lemon. She stretched herself and yawned and listened as she heard steps on the ladder and her uncle's panting as he climbed.

"Did you buy me a bathing suit, Félice?" she called.

Her maid's voice rose from the ladder.

"Ah no, ma'moselle. The store said he had no call for Ma'moselle's kind."

Then Mr Farnam, Mr. Farnam's head appeared, and after him Félice. He nodded at her coldly.

"You won't need a bathing suit;" he said, "we're starting north right away."

"Oh, shut up!" ~~said~~ suggested Ardita from sheer force of habit. She turned to her maid.

"Félice," she ~~said~~ demanded, "was it you who told me you'd seen a wonderful vaudeville act last spring called Curtis Carlyle and his Six ~~Brown~~ Black Buddies?"

"Yes -- Ma'moselle, ah, it was truly marvelous --"

"Tell me," interrupted Ardita eagerly, "was Curtis Carlyle a dark-haired young man with blue eyes - very good looking?"

"Oh, no, Ma'moselle. Oh, no! He is small and ugly as sinning. He has grey hair and his legs they are bow-legged."

"Hm," remarked Ardita thoughtfully. "It's a darn funny world, isn't it, Felice?"

"Oh, yes," ~~replied~~ agreed Félice, "It's a darn funny world."

50. Lobby still for *The Husband Hunter* (Fox Entertainment, 1920).

Fitzgerald sold the movie rights to "Myra Meets His Family" (*The Saturday Evening Post*, March 20, 1920) for $1,000. The original story portrays an aging debutante's effort to snare a rich husband. Her intended groom realizes that he has been tricked into an unwanted engagement and stages an elaborate scheme to scare her off. He hires actors to portray mentally unbalanced parents and reveals a racially mixed heritage. The lobby still depicts the story's comic climax.

51. Lobby poster for *The Off-Shore Pirate* (Metro Pictures Corporation, 1921).

Fitzgerald sold the story's film rights for $3,000 to Metro Pictures Corporation. Throughout his career Fitzgerald sought and encouraged stage and film treatments of his fiction, not only for the extra income generated but also for the exposure of his work and name. Fitzgerald's awareness of his work as a commodity can be seen in his *Ledger*, in which he recorded the sale of each story, novel, play, and article.

The poster features Viola Dana and Jack Mulhall as the kidnapped heiress and hijacker (see color insert). Fitzgerald's comic stories of young love and imaginative schemes perfectly suited the early 1920s film market. Because of the fragile and flammable nitrate film, none of the early silent movies based on Fitzgerald's stories survives. See color insert.

52. *Flappers and Philosophers* (New York: Scribners, 1920).

Scribners published Fitzgerald's first story collection soon after the success of *This Side of Paradise* in order to keep the author's name before the book-buying public. The cover exploits Fitzgerald's recent magazine success by illustrating "Bernice Bobs Her Hair," one of the author's most popular *Post* stories (May 1, 1920). The story demonstrates how Fitzgerald could craft a controversial story to fit the *Post*'s conservative criteria. In the early 1920s teenage girls disobeyed and shocked the older generation by cutting their hair mannishly short. Despite the title Bernice does not bob her hair out of rebellion but rather as the result of a trick. See color insert.

Fitzgerald based this story on his own letter of advice to his sister Annabel in 1915. As in his fiction, Fitzgerald describes women's charm in martial terms. He urges his sister to practice her smile continually because "when you've practiced a thing in calm, then only are you sure of it as a good weapon in tight places" (*Life in Letters*, p. 8).

53. George Barton, *The Bell Haven Eight* (Philadelphia: Winston, 1914), inscribed to Harold Ober, n.d.

Fitzgerald humorously inscribed this volume of prep school stories to his literary agent and Harvard graduate Harold Ober. During their twenty-one-year association Ober served as Fitzgerald's agent, accountant, banker, confidant, friend, and surrogate parent to his daughter. In expectation of a magazine sale Ober often advanced Fitzgerald money on the receipt of a story. As Fitzgerald's stories became harder to place in the mid-1930s, Ober's advances became noninterest loans. By 1937 Fitzgerald owed Ober more than $12,000. While under contract to M-G-M, Fitzgerald repaid his debt within two years. Fitzgerald dedicated his fourth and final story collection, *Taps at Reveille*, to Ober.

54. "The Rich Boy," *The Red Book Magazine* (January and February 1926).

Fitzgerald believed that his novella would face obstacles in a commercial market because of its length and tragic theme. Stories of more than 10,000 words were difficult to place in magazines because they often required two issues. But Ober pursued a high-circulation venue for the story and succeeded in selling it to *Red Book* after rejection by the *Post*. *Red Book*, a *Post* competitor, prominently advertised the story on its cover as "A great story of today's youth by F. Scott Fitzgerald."

Because many of the slicks represented conservative American traditions, sometimes to the extent of xenophobia, the *Red Book* editors felt compelled to defend Fitzgerald's foreign residence. As a celebrity, Fitzgerald received a large amount of publicity. In the story's second installment, *Red Book* provided the following headnote:

> F. Scott Fitzgerald is one of the constantly increasing number of American writers and artists living abroad. But for all that, the author of "The Great Gatsby," "This Side of Paradise," and the present story, writes only of Americans as they appear against their natural background. The so-called European "taint," even in the manner of his writing, has never appeared, nor is it at all likely to (75).

The story contains Fitzgerald's most quoted and misquoted sentences:
"Let me tell you about the very rich. They are different from you and me."

55. F. Scott Fitzgerald and family, 1925 passport.

From spring 1924 to 1931 the Fitzgeralds lived mostly abroad. Although he associated with the literary expatriate group that included Ernest Hemingway, his fiction remained strongly tied to American values and ideals. His stories set abroad portray Europe as a corrupting agent, conducive to moral dissipation and disastrous for Americans.

Beginning with "Love in the Night" (*The Saturday Evening Post*, March 14, 1925) Fitzgerald began to write stories with foreign settings. Parisian cafes and Swiss hotels became such frequent settings for Fitzgerald's fiction that in 1931 the *Post* editors complained to Ober that they wanted "American stories— that is stories laid on this side of the Atlantic" (*As Ever, Scott Fitz—*, p. 176).

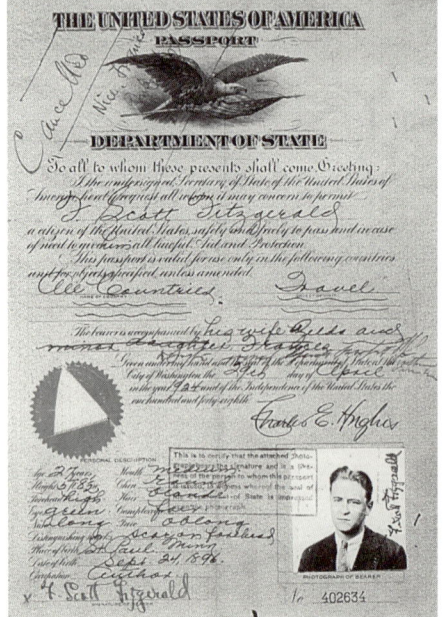
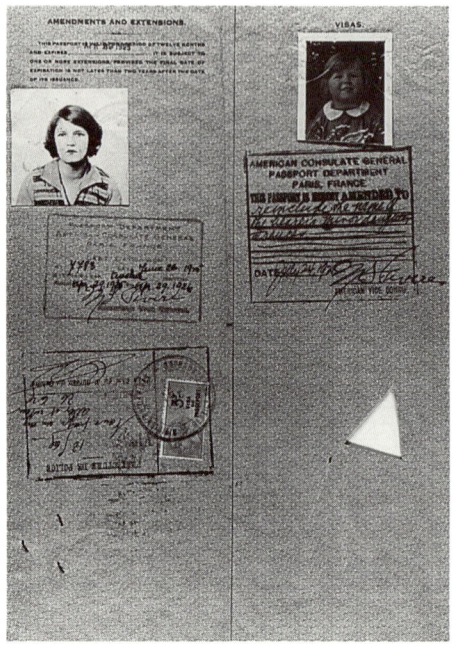

56. *This Side of Paradise* (New York: Scribners, 1920), inscribed to Lois Moran, c. 1927; "Jacob's Ladder," *The Saturday Evening Post* (August 20, 1927); photograph of Lois Moran, autographed.

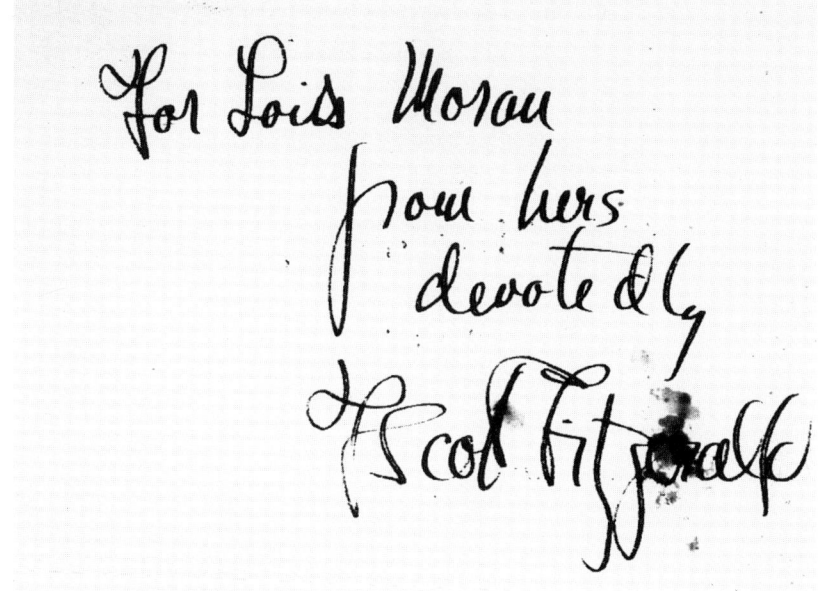

During a 1927 trip to Hollywood Fitzgerald met actress Lois Moran. She had made a successful American debut as the ingenue in *Stella Dallas* (1925). Fitzgerald was attracted to the young actress and performed with her in a screen test. During an argument over Fitzgerald's interest in Moran, Zelda Fitzgerald threw her wristwatch from a train.

Fitzgerald drew on his relationship with Lois Moran for "Jacob's Ladder." In 1927 the *Post* paid $3,000 for the story, raising Fitzgerald's price $500. It was Fitzgerald's first *Post* appearance in more than a year, and the magazine placed it first in the issue. In the story an older man helps a beautiful young girl become a movie star. Although she is grateful to her patron, she does not love him.

Moran also provided the model for Rosemary Hoyt in *Tender Is the Night*. In a 1935 letter to Moran, Fitzgerald explains why he had not included "Jacob's Ladder" in his latest short-story collection: "I found that I had so thoroughly disemboweled it of its best descriptions for 'Tender is the Night' that it would be offering an empty shell" (*Correspondence*, p. 403).

57. *Taps at Reveille* (New York: Scribners, 1935), inscribed to Tony Buttitta, 1935.

Tony Buttitta operated a bookshop in Asheville, N.C., where he developed a friendly acquaintance with Fitzgerald. In Buttitta's copy of *Taps at Reveille,* Fitzgerald marked out a paragraph from "Babylon Revisited" that he had harvested from the story for use in *Tender Is the Night*. Fitzgerald often gleaned descriptions and scenes from magazine stories for his novels. If he chose the story to be collected in a volume, he would remove the portions that he "stripped" for his novels. In a 1935 letter to Maxwell Perkins, Fitzgerald noted this specific repetition in "Babylon Revisited": "Just found another whole paragraph in 'Taps,' top of page 384, which appears in 'Tender is the Night.' I'd carefully elided it and written the paragraph beneath it to replace it, but the proof readers slipped and put them both in" (*Life in Letters*, p. 279).

"Babylon Revisited," one of Fitzgerald's most-celebrated stories, appeared in *The Saturday Evening Post* (February 21, 1931), which placed it first in the issue. On its surface this story of a reformed alcoholic widower trying to regain custody of his daughter in Depression-era Paris would not appear to conform to the *Post*'s wholesome image. Yet the story does fulfill the *Post*'s moral requirements. Although the hero exhibits a noble purpose in trying to reform so that he can win back his child, he cannot escape his indirect responsibility for his wife's death. Charlie Wales remains haunted by his reckless behavior, remembering "The men who locked their wives out in the snow, because the snow of twenty-nine wasn't real snow. If you didn't want it to be snow you just paid some money" (see item 92).

In his assessment of *Post* editor George Horace Lorimer, Fitzgerald explained how a tragic story might meet the magazine's requirement for optimism: "He made a sharp distinction between a sordid tragedy and a heroic tragedy—hating the former but accepting the latter as an essential and interesting part of life" (*Life in Letters*, p. 633).

58. "The Count of Darkness," RTS, 39 pp.; "The Kingdom in the Dark," RTS, 53 pp.; "The Count of Darkness," *Redbook Magazine* (June 1935).

In an unsuccessful effort to write a magazine series that could be combined later into a novel, Fitzgerald began a medieval adventure serial featuring Philippe, Count of Darkness. A lifelong history enthusiast, Fitzgerald attempted to narrate the birth of the European feudal system. He modeled his young hero on Ernest Hemingway. Although Fitzgerald wrote this story during his decline as a magazine writer, the typescript illustrates that the author revised his text with the same level of attention to detail and style as he had always exerted.

The Philippe series was bought by *Redbook*, and the first installment, "In the Darkest Hour," appeared in October 1934 with the story's title and Fitzgerald's name appearing on the cover. The headnote for the second installment, "Count of Darkness," deliberately invokes Fitzgerald's literary reputation. It also inadvertently reveals the absurdity of the series by connecting Fitzgerald's prestige as a social realist with a story of medieval adventure: "The brilliant thought quality and style of the creator of 'The Great Gatsby' are very much in evidence in this majestic story of 819 A.D."

Redbook abandoned the series after three installments. The magazine published the fourth story, "Gods of Darkness," in November 1941, eleven months after Fitzgerald's death.

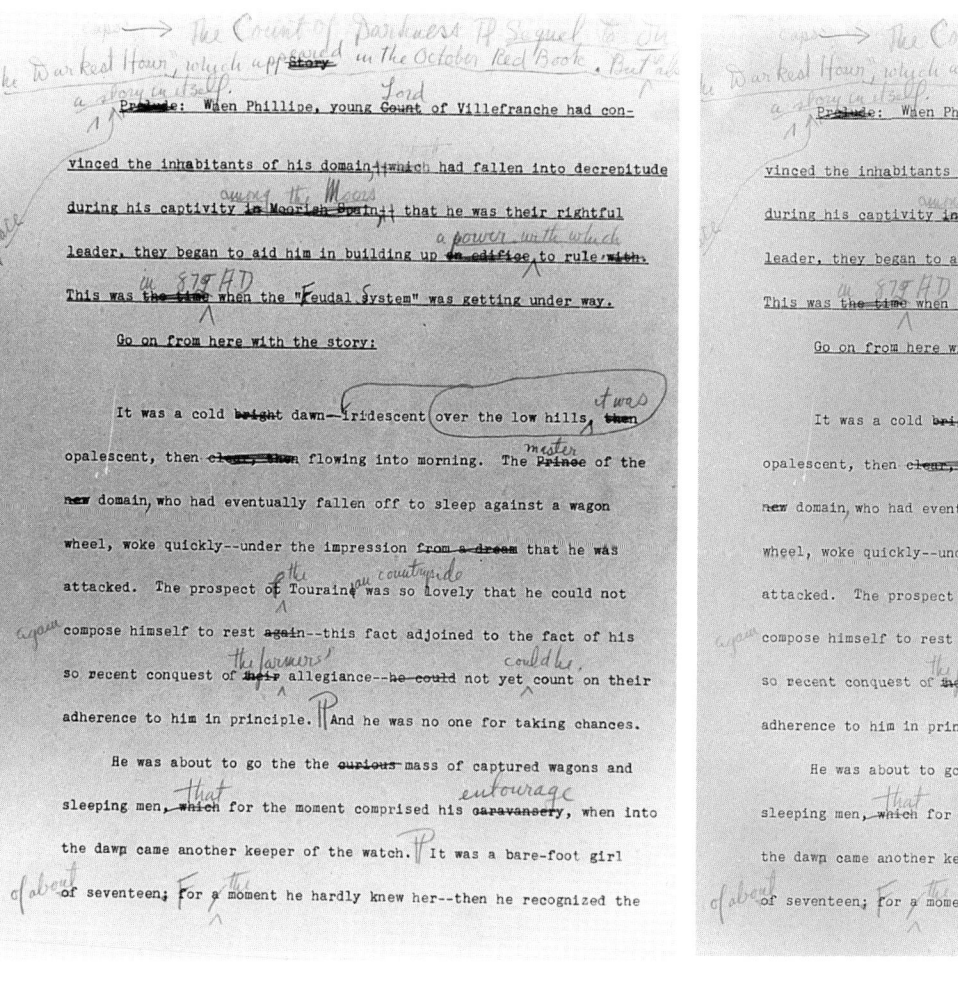

59. *Taps at Reveille* (New York: Scribners, 1935), inscribed to Annah Williamson, 1936.

During his "Crack-Up" period Fitzgerald inscribed a copy of his last short-story collection, *Taps at Reveille*, for a relative of Dorothy Williamson, his private nurse in Asheville, N.C. See color insert.

The inscription can be read as Fitzgerald's defense of his short stories and the personal material upon which they drew. Although Fitzgerald disparaged his magazine fiction to other writers, he shared perhaps his most revealing evaluation of his stories with only himself. In his *Notebooks* Fitzgerald recorded:

> "I have asked a lot of my emotions—one hundred and twenty stories. The price was high, right up with Kipling, because there was one little drop of something not blood, not a tear, not my seed, but me more intimately than these, in every story, it was the extra I had. Now it has gone and I am just like you now" (*Notebooks*, p. 131).

An American Man of Letters

by Robert F. Moss

In both scholarly studies and popular legend, F. Scott Fitzgerald has been characterized as a careless, "natural" writer who spent more time at parties than at work on his fiction. What has often been missed is that Fitzgerald was an active and influential American man of letters. The term "man of letters" refers not to the private activities of an author—his writing, his reading, and his literary ideas—but rather to his public role as a literary figure: his critical reputation, his relationships with and influence on other writers, his efforts to encourage writers, and his sense of his own place in the literature of his time. The career of F. Scott Fitzgerald meets all these criteria. He was well-connected in the literary world, establishing friendships with and gaining the admiration of some of the most influential writers of the 1920s and 1930s. As a book reviewer and a self-appointed talent scout for Charles Scribner's Sons, he helped to promote the careers of other writers—most notably Ernest Hemingway and Ring Lardner. The holdings of the Bruccoli Collection at the University of South Carolina demonstrate F. Scott Fitzgerald's achievement as an American man of letters.

The publication of *This Side of Paradise* (1920) established the basic patterns for how Fitzgerald would be perceived throughout his career. The sensational material in the novel—the behavior of rebellious young women and questing collegians—caused him to be identified as a spokesman for the younger generation and created the expectation that he would continue to probe and exploit the subjects of love, sex, and marriage among the young. Despite his being labeled "the chronicler of the flapper," Fitzgerald's young women were neither frivolous nor insubstantial. They were instead tough-minded and independent, defying convention and engaging in determined efforts to make strong marriages. As such, Fitzgerald's female characters were controversial and established for him a reputation as a daring, iconoclastic author. He enjoyed his early celebrity and, through a series of interviews and public statements, adopted the persona of a brash young genius. Fitzgerald and his wife, Zelda, were both young and attractive, and these characteristics, combined with public antics such as riding atop taxicabs and jumping into fountains, contributed to his reputation for frivolity.

This period of early success was not solely a time of parties and carousing. From the beginning of his career Fitzgerald established and maintained friendships with important members of the American literary community—including Edmund Wilson, John Peale Bishop, H. L. Mencken, George Jean Nathan, and John Dos Passos. In 1922 he recommended Woodward Boyd's *The Love Legend* and Thomas Boyd's *Through the Wheat* to Scribners and, following their publication, reviewed both novels for the *New York Evening Post*. Fitzgerald also brought Ring Lardner to Scribners and helped plan Lardner's collection *How to Write Short Stories*. Other books reviewed by Fitzgerald between 1920 and 1924 include Mencken's *Prejudices: Second Series*, Booth Tarkington's *Gentle Julia*, John Dos Passos's *Three Soldiers*, Shane Leslie's *The Oppidan,* and Sherwood Anderson's *Many Marriages*. These reviews paid only three to five dollars each; Fitzgerald was writing them not for financial reasons but because he was dedicated to promoting writing he found worthwhile. Further evidence of Fitzgerald's involvement in the American literary world during the early years of his career is provided by books in the Bruccoli Collection that are inscribed to Fitzgerald by Thomas Beer, James Branch Cabell, Samuel Hopkins Adams ("Warner Fabian"), Donald Ogden Stewart, and Carl Van Vechten.

Fitzgerald's literary connections were increased in 1924, when he left America for France and completed his third novel, *The Great Gatsby* (1925). Although the sales of the novel were disappointing, some reviewers praised him as one of America's most promising writers. "Fitzgerald," Gilbert Seldes wrote, "has more than matured. He has mastered his talents and gone soaring in a beautiful flight, leaving behind him everything dubious and tricky in his earlier work, and leaving even farther behind his own generation and most of his elders" (*Critical Reception,* p. 239). Fitzgerald was not a true member of the expatriate literary scene in France: he was not an experimentalist and did not write for the little magazines. His writing was too developed and his sensibility too American to be influenced by his years in Europe. Fitzgerald was, nevertheless, admired by members of the expatriate American literary community. Materials in the Bruccoli Collection document Fitzgerald's relationships with major figures such as Gertrude Stein, James Joyce, T. S. Eliot, and—most notably—Ernest Hemingway.

The friendship with Hemingway is the best example of Fitzgerald's functioning as a man of letters. Even before they met, Fitzgerald was aware of Hemingway's writing and recommended him to Maxwell Perkins as a promising author Scribners should publish. After their first meeting at the Dingo bar in Paris in May 1925, Fitzgerald acted as an intermediary between Scribners and Hemingway, who had already signed a three-book contract with Boni & Liveright. When Boni & Liveright rejected *The Torrents of Spring* (1926), a parody of Sherwood Anderson, Fitzgerald assisted in the negotiations to secure Hemingway as a Scribners author. Fitzgerald read and evaluated the manuscript for *The Sun Also Rises* (1926), producing a ten-page report that led Hemingway to excise the first chapter of the novel. In 1929 he made similar recommendations for Hemingway's second novel, *A Farewell to Arms.* Fitzgerald also wrote an essay-review of *In Our Time* (1925) for the May 1926 *Bookman* in which he praised Hemingway as a writer to be watched. Fitzgerald played a key role in launching Hemingway's career as a novelist, and their friendship would continue—albeit with strain—until Fitzgerald's death in 1940, becoming the most celebrated American literary friendship of the 20th century.

Fitzgerald continued to act as a man of letters throughout his lifetime. In Hollywood during the late 1930s he met and became friends with some of the younger fiction writers, including Nathanael West, S. J. Perelman, and Budd Schulberg. Fitzgerald wrote dustjacket blurbs for West's *Day of the Locust,* Schulberg's *What Makes Sammy Run,* and Arnold Gingrich's *Cast Down the Laurel*. But his public role was not limited to fostering individual authors. He was actively concerned with the condition of American fiction and its future. Fitzgerald's book reviews, essays, and interviews encouraged the use of American material and themes, genuine emotion, and purified style. They show his involvement in and response to the efforts during the 1920s and 1930s to reshape and reinvigorate American literature. F. Scott Fitzgerald was not the undisciplined "natural" of legend but rather a dedicated and influential American man of letters.

◆ ◆ ◆

60. "The Author's Apology," *This Side of Paradise* **(New York: Scribners, 1920)—third printing, April 1920.**

This statement was tipped into copies of the third printing of *This Side of Paradise* for distribution at the May 1920 convention of the American Booksellers Association. It shows Fitzgerald's public pose at the beginning of his career: that of young author/genius. Fitzgerald connects his writing of the novel with the beginning of Prohibition, which went into effect 1 July 1919. Although his statement portrays the composition of *This Side of Paradise* as being rapid, he actually began writing the novel in November 1917 and—after having it twice rejected by Scribners—began rewriting it in July 1919. The novel was accepted for publication in September.

Copyright by White

The Author's Apology

I don't want to talk about myself because I'll admit I did that somewhat in this book. In fact, to write it took three months; to conceive it—three minutes; to collect the data in it—all my life. The idea of writing it came on the first of last July: it was a substitute form of dissipation.

My whole theory of writing I can sum up in one sentence: An author ought to write for the youth of his own generation, the critics of the next, and the schoolmasters of ever afterward.

So, gentlemen, consider all the cocktails mentioned in this book drunk by me as a toast to the American Booksellers Association.

MAY, 1920

Sincerely
Scott Fitzgerald

61. John Dos Passos, *A Pushcart at the Curb* (New York: Doran, 1922), inscribed by Dos Passos on free front endpaper.

In fall 1922, not long after their first meeting, Dos Passos accompanied the Fitzgeralds on a trip to Long Island to go house hunting. During the ride the two authors discussed writing, and Dos Passos was surprised by the quality of Fitzgerald's literary ideas: "When he talked about writing his mind, which seemed to me full of preposterous notions about most things, became clear and hard as a diamond. . . . about writing he was a born professional. Everything he said was worth listening to" (*Best Times*, p. 146). Fitzgerald was an admirer of Dos Passos's writing. Fitzgerald reviewed Dos Passos's *Three Soldiers* for the *St. Paul Daily News* (September 25, 1921)—possibly before they met—and later praised the novel in "How to Waste Material: A Note on My Generation."

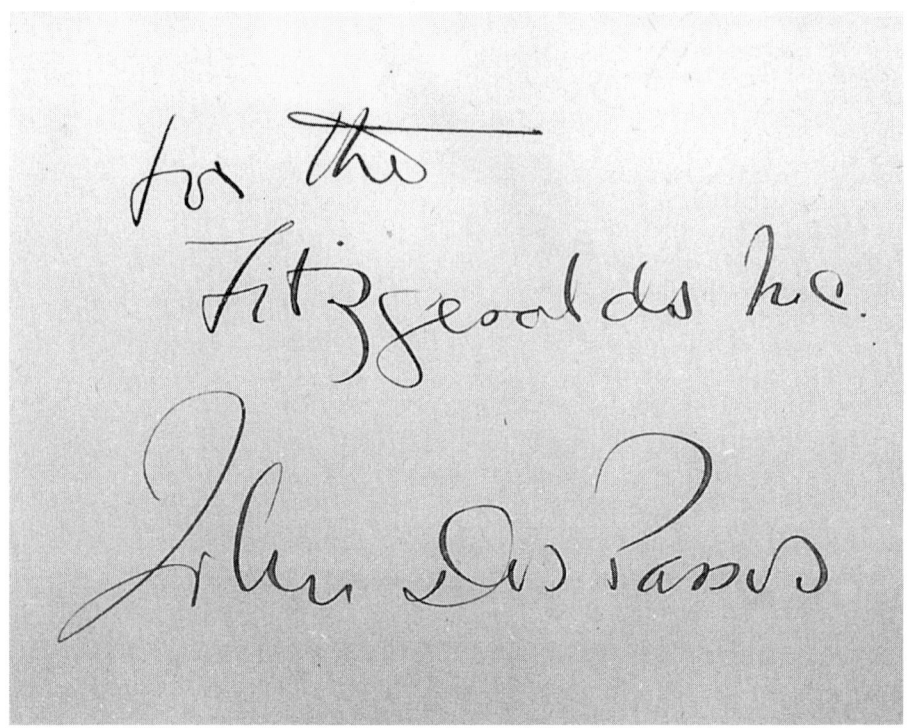

62. Thomas Boyd, *Through the Wheat* (New York: Scribners, 1923), inscribed by Boyd on free front endpaper.

Fitzgerald met Boyd in St. Paul in summer 1921. Boyd, then the literary editor of the *St. Paul Daily News*, was an aspiring novelist. Fitzgerald gave advice on *Through the Wheat*, Boyd's first novel, and recommended it to editor Maxwell Perkins for publication by Scribners. Fitzgerald also recommended *The Love Legend*, the first novel by Boyd's wife Peggy, who wrote under the name Woodward Boyd. The two novels provide early instances of Fitzgerald's acting as a self-appointed talent scout for Scribners, an integral part of his role as a man of letters.

63. Ring W. Lardner, *How to Write Short Stories* (New York: Scribners, 1924): Fitzgerald's copy with holograph annotations.

After moving to Great Neck, Long Island, in fall 1922, Fitzgerald became friends with Ring Lardner. Lardner was a successful newspaper columnist and magazine writer, but his short-story volumes had yet to reach a wide audience. Fitzgerald introduced Lardner to Maxwell Perkins and provided the title *How to Write Short Stories*. The volume was published in 1924 and led to a reevaluation of Lardner's work. He remained a Scribners author, publishing six more volumes and a collected edition with the firm. Fitzgerald wrote "Read Golden Honeymoon" on the recto of the free front endpaper of this copy and on the verso added a list of other Lardner books. Fitzgerald's holograph annotations on the contents page are apparently his ranking of the stories in the collection.

64. Ring Lardner, TS, 1 p., with Fitzgerald's holograph note.

The Lardner-Fitzgerald friendship continued after the Fitzgeralds left Great Neck, and the two writers exchanged Christmas poems. The character Abe North in *Tender Is the Night* was modeled on Lardner.

Fitzgerald replied:

You combed Third Avenue last year
   For some small gift that was not to dear
  --Like a candy cane or a worn out truss--
  To give to a loving friend like us
You'd found gold eggs for such wealthy hicks
   As the Edsell Fords and the Pittsburgh Fricks
The Andy Mellons, the Teddy Shonts
   The Coleman T. and Pierre duPonts
But not one gift to brighten our hoem
  --So I'm sending you back your God damn poem.

```
                        COPY

We combed Fifth Avenue this last month
A hundred times if we combed it onth,
In search of something we thought would do
To give to a person as nice as you.


We had no trouble selecting gifts
For the Ogden Armours and Louie Swifts,
The Otto Kahns and the George E. Bakers,
The Munns and the Rodman Wanamakers.


It's a simple matter to pick things out
For people one isn't so wild about,
But you, you wonderful pal and friend, you!
We couldn't find anything fit to send you.

                             THE RING LARDNERS
```

Xmas 1927 or 1928
I forget which

65. *The Great Gatsby* (New York: Scribners, 1925), first printing inscribed to Van Wyck Brooks on slip pasted to free front endpaper.

Fitzgerald was in Europe when *The Great Gatsby* was published. He sent handwritten slips to Maxwell Perkins to be inserted in presentation copies of the novel, including this one for Van Wyck Brooks, an influential American critic and literary historian. Brooks responded in a April 22, 1925, letter, "I have just read it, with the greatest delights, and it seems to me by far the best thing you've done—certainly a real creation and one that leaves in the mind a most haunting impression" (*Correspondence*, p. 160).

66. Van Wyck Brooks, *The Ordeal of Mark Twain* (New York: Dutton, 1920): Fitzgerald's copy, signed by him on free front endpaper.

67. Van Wyck Brooks, *The Pilgrimage of Henry James* (New York: Dutton, 1925), inscribed by Brooks.

After receiving an inscribed copy of *The Great Gatsby* from Fitzgerald, Brooks reciprocated with this inscribed copy of his critical study of Henry James.

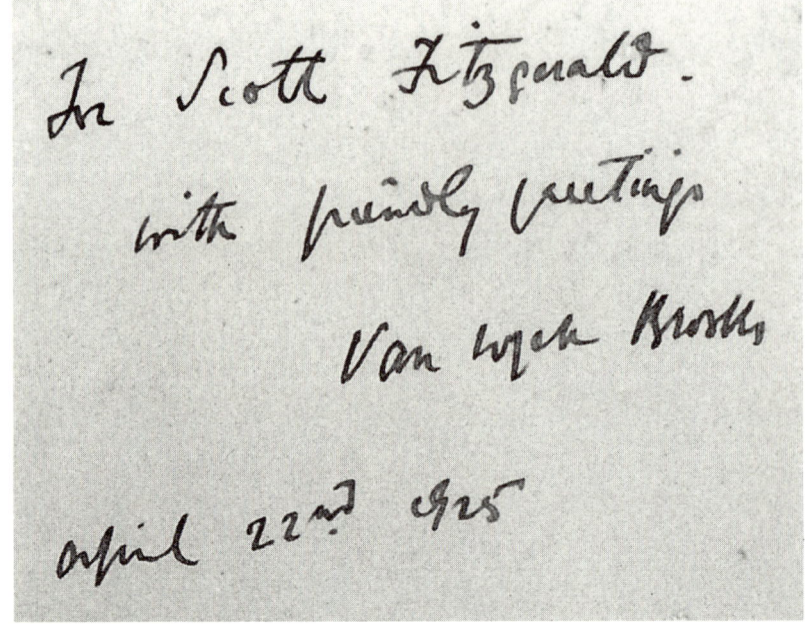

Gordon Bryant's portrait of F. Scott Fitzgerald, 1921 (Arlyn Bruccoli Collection).

Gordon Bryant's portrait of Zelda Fitzgerald, 1921 (Arlyn Bruccoli Collection).

Acting script for Fitzgerald's 1914 Triangle Club musical.

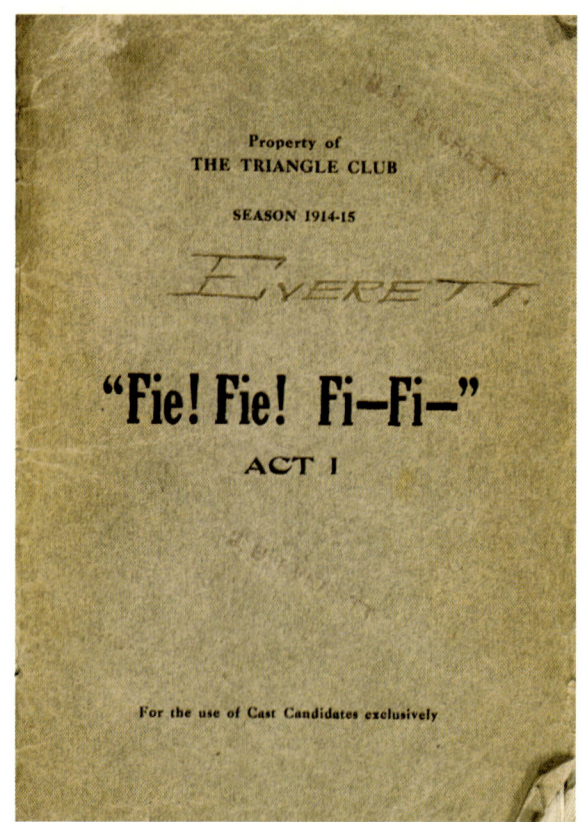

Score for Fitzgerald's 1914 Triangle Club musical.

Score for Fitzgerald's 1915 Triangle Club musical.

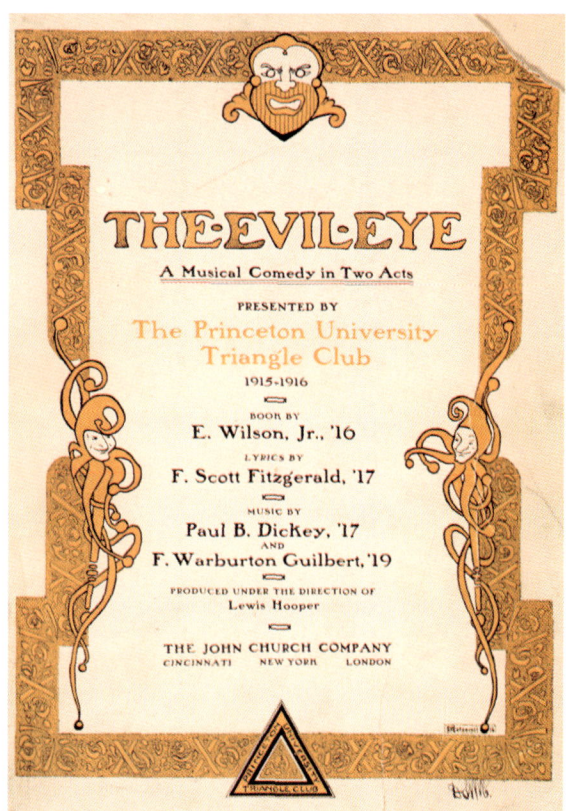

Score for Fitzgerald's 1916 Triangle Club musical.

Dust jacket for Fitzgerald's first novel, 1920.

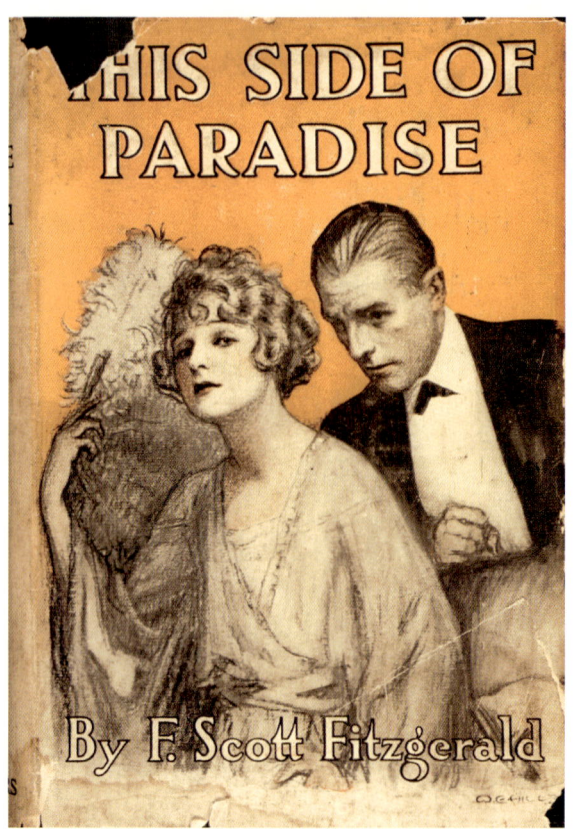

Dust jacket for Fitzgerald's first story collection, 1920.

Lobby poster for the 1921 movie based on Fitzgerald's story (Arlyn Bruccoli Collection)

Cover for the first installment of *The Beautiful and Damned*, serialized from September 1921 through March 1922.

Dust jacket for Fitzgerald's second novel, 1922.

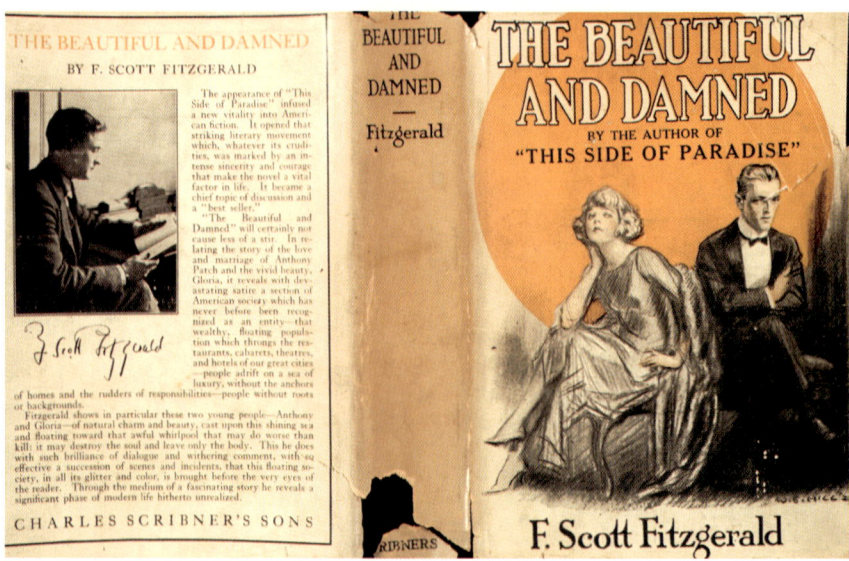

John Held, Jr.'s dust jacket for Fitzgerald's second story collection, 1922.

Cover for the first publication of Fitzgerald's short story.

John Held, Jr.'s dust jacket for Fitzgerald's only published play, 1923.

Francis Cugat's painting of the Valley of the Ashes (Arlyn Bruccoli Collection).

Cugat's preliminary sketch for the *Gatsby* dust jacket (Arlyn Bruccoli Collection).

Cugat's final sketch for the *Gatsby* dust jacket (Arlyn Bruccoli Collection).

Cugat painted a duplicate of the final *Gatsby* jacket art for his own collection (Arlyn Bruccoli Collection).

Dust jacket for Fitzgerald's third novel, 1925.

Remainder dust jacket for the 1926 English printing.

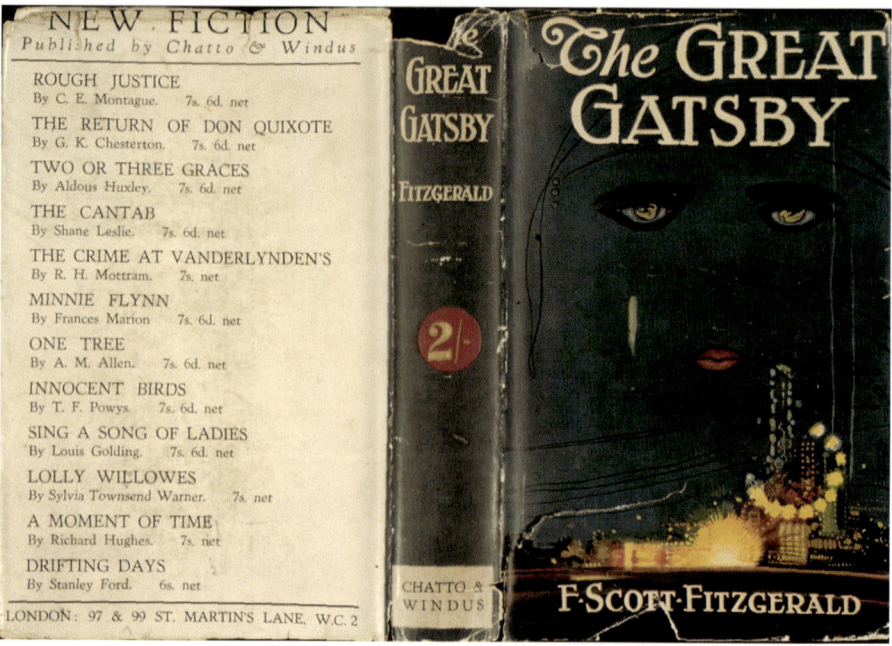

Poster for the 1949 Paramount movie (Arlyn Bruccoli Collection).

Dust jacket for Fitzgerald's third story collection, 1926.

Cover for the first installment of *Tender Is the Night*, serialized from January through April 1934.

Dust jacket for Fitzgerald's fourth novel, 1934.

Dust jacket for Fitzgerald's fourth story collection, 1935.

Dust jacket for Fitzgerald's posthumously published novel-in-progress, 1941.

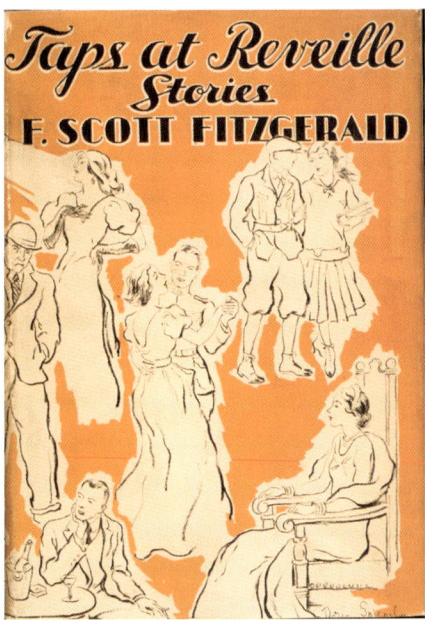
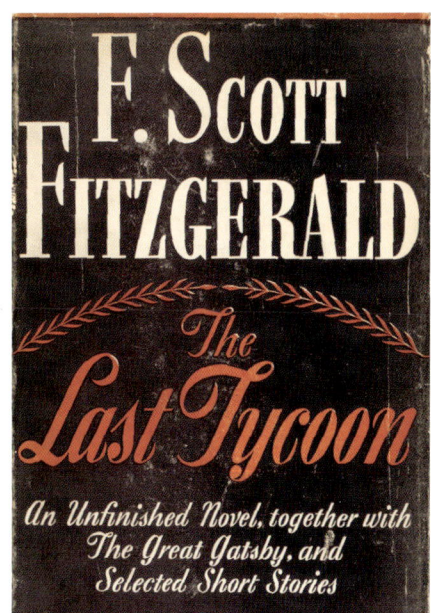

Poster for the 1938 movie that earned Fitzgerald his only screen credit (Arlyn Bruccoli Collection).

Dust jacket for Zelda Fitzgerald's only published book, 1932.

Zelda Fitzgerald's untitled gouache painting of dancers (Arlyn Bruccoli Collection).

Zelda Fitzgerald's gouache painting of "The Lobster Quadrille" (Arlyn Bruccoli Collection).

Fitzgerald's postcards to Scottie.

Flask presented to Fitzgerald by Montgomery friends in 1918.

Fitzgerald's briefcase.

68. Fitzgerald to Van Wyck Brooks, June 13, 1925, Paris, ALS, 1 p.

Fitzgerald responded to Brooks's gift of *The Pilgrimage of Henry James* with this letter championing American themes and material and expressing his conviction that writers' sensibilities are ultimately determined by their experiences before the age of twenty-one.

> 14 Rue de Tilsitt
> Paris, France
> June 13, 1925
>
> Dear Brooks:
>
> I read the James book, so did Zelda & Ernest Hemmingway + everyone I've been able to lend it to and I think it rises high above either Bunny's carping or Seldes' tag on it. I like it even better than the Mark Twain. It is exquisitely done + entirely fascinating.
>
> One reason it is of particular interest to us over here is obvious. In my own case I have no such delicate doubts — nor does anyone need to have them now since the American scene has become so complicated + ramified but the question of material (freshening) always exists. I shall come back after one more novel.
>
> Why didn't you touch more on James impotence (physical) and its influence? I think if he hadn't had at least one poignant emotional love affair with an American girl on American soil he might have lived there twice as long, tried twice as hard, had the picaresque part of Huck Finn + yet never struck roots. Novelists like he (him) + in a sense (to descend a good bit) me, have to have love as a main concern since our interest lies outside the economic struggle or the life of violence, as conditioned to some extent by our lives from 16–21.
>
> However this is just shooting in the dark at a target on which you have expended your fine talent in full daylight. It was a really thrilling pleasure for a writer to read. Thanking you for writing me about my book so kindly + for sending me yours.
>
> Scott Fitzgerald

69. Lawrence Leighton, "An Autopsy and a Prescription," *Hound and Horn* (1932), with annotations by Fitzgerald.

Leighton's essay condemned the work of Fitzgerald, John Dos Passos, and Ernest Hemingway as "repulsive, sterile, and dead" and claimed that they had turned their backs on the American novelistic tradition. Fitzgerald's marginal annotations give his responses to Leighton's charges.

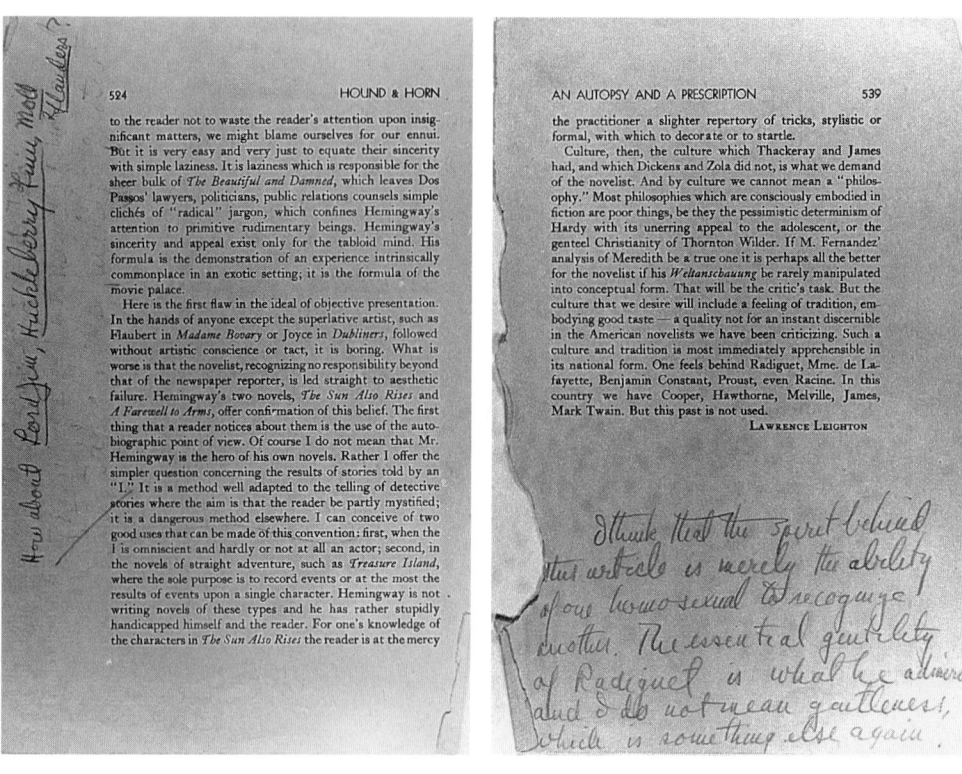

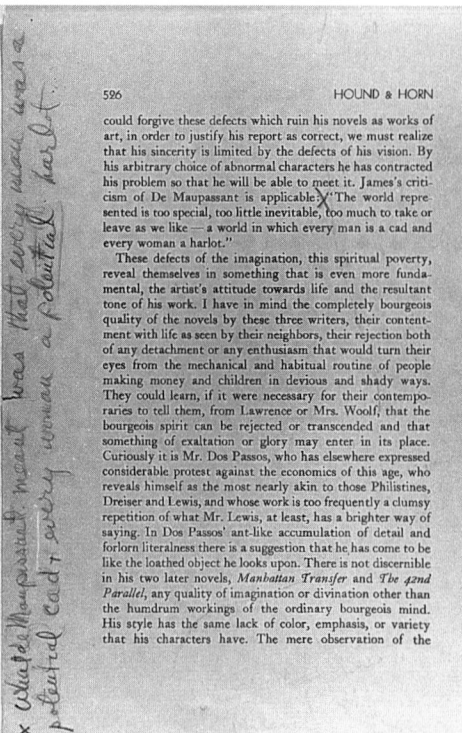

70. Ernest Hemingway to Grace Hemingway, October 19, 1925, Paris, ALS 1 p.; Fitzgerald, "How to Waste Material: A Note on My Generation," *The Bookman* (May 1926).

Hemingway's claim to his mother that he was giving boxing lessons to Fitzgerald is unsubstantiated. Hemingway's exaggeration and self-promotion colored his later accounts of his relationship with Fitzgerald, such as *A Moveable Feast* (1964). In 1925 Hemingway was a fledgling writer who had yet to publish a novel. Fitzgerald recruited Hemingway for Scribners. In his *Bookman* essay/review, Fitzgerald assesses the failure of American writers to use American material and says of *In Our Time* (1925), "many of us who have grown weary of admonitions to watch this man or that have felt a sort of renewal of excitement at these stories wherein Ernest Hemingway turns a corner into the street" (*Miscellany*, p. 149).

71. Photograph of Ernest Hemingway, inscribed by Hemingway: "To Scott from his old bedfellow Richard Halliburton, Princeton 1931."

Halliburton was a Princetonian and a well-known lecturer and writer of adventure travelogues. The inscription refers to Halliburton's alleged homosexuality.

72. Ernest Hemingway, *For Whom the Bell Tolls* (New York: Scribners, 1940)—1st printing, inscribed by Hemingway on free front endpaper.

The relationship between Fitzgerald and Hemingway was damaged by Hemingway's condescending reference to "poor Scott Fitzgerald" and his awe of the rich in "The Snows of Kilimanjaro" (*Esquire,* August 1936). The two writers' last meeting was in 1937, but this volume provides evidence of Hemingway's continuing affection for Fitzgerald (see item 25). Fitzgerald wrote of *For Whom the Bell Tolls,* "It is so to speak Ernest's 'Tale of Two Cities' though the comparison isn't apt. I mean it is a thoroughly superficial book which has all the profundity of Rebecca" (*Notebooks,* p. 335).

73. James Joyce, *Ulysses* (Paris: Shakespeare & Co., 1922); Joyce to Fitzgerald, July 11, 1928, Paris, ALS, 1 p., pasted on free front endpaper.

Fitzgerald first met Joyce on June 27, 1926, at one of Sylvia Beach's dinner parties in Paris. At this meeting Fitzgerald reportedly upset Joyce by offering to leap from a sixth-floor window as a gesture of admiration. Joyce's note reads, "Dear Mr. Fitzgerald: Here with is the book you gave me signed and I am adding a portrait of the artist as a once young man with the thanks of your much obliged but most pusillanimous guest."

74. James Joyce, *A Portrait of the Artist as a Young Man* (London: Cape, 1926), inscribed by Joyce on free front endpaper: "To / Scott Fitzgerald / James Joyce / Paris / 11-7-1928."

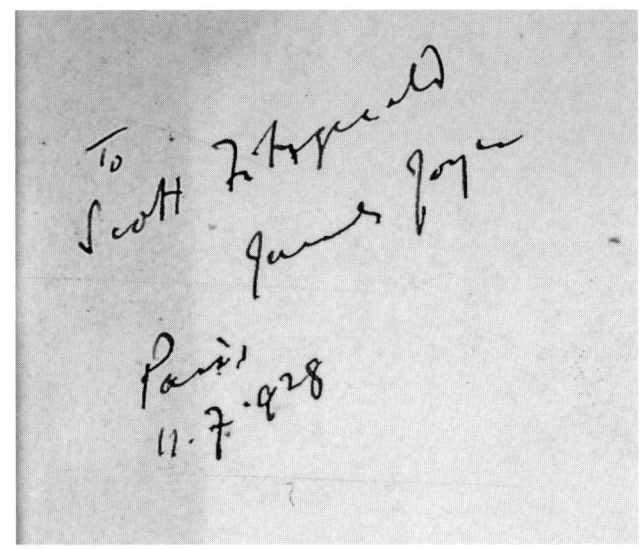

75. James Joyce, *Gens de Dublin [Dubliners]* (Paris: Librairie Plon, 1926), inscribed by Fitzgerald to René Crevel on free front endpaper.

Crevel was a French novelist whom Fitzgerald met in Paris. In a January 21, 1930, letter to Maxwell Perkins, Fitzgerald wrote, "In the foreign (French) field there is besides Chamson one man, and at the opposite pole, of great great talent. It is not Cocteau nor Arragon but young *René Crevel*" (*Life in Letters*, p. 176).

76. T. S. Eliot, *Ash Wednesday* (London: Faber & Faber, 1930), inscribed by Eliot on title page.

Although they did not meet until February 1933, when Eliot lectured on the Metaphysical poets at Johns Hopkins University and inscribed this volume, the two writers had long admired each other's work. Fitzgerald drew upon Eliot's *The Waste Land* (1922) for the Valley of Ashes in *The Great Gatsby* and inscribed a copy of the novel, "For T.S. Eliott / Greatest of Living Poets / from his entheusiastic / worshipper / F. Scott Fitzgerald" (*Correspondence*, p. 180). In a 1925 letter to Fitzgerald, Eliot called *Gatsby*, "the first step American fiction has taken since Henry James" (*Crack-Up*, p. 310).

77. Gertrude Stein, *How to Write* (Paris: Plain Edition, 1931), inscribed by Stein: "To Fitzgerald and I hope you did not mind my putting you in here."

On page 30 Fitzgerald underlined the phrase, "That is the cruelest thing I ever heard," apparently indicating the reference in Stein's inscription. He was introduced to Stein by Ernest Hemingway in 1925. Fitzgerald never became a follower of her theories, but Stein praised his writing. Of *The Great Gatsby* she wrote, "[I]t is a good book. I like the melody of your dedication it shows that you have a background of beauty and tenderness and that is a comfort. The next good thing is that you write naturally in sentences and that too is a comfort" (*Crack-Up*, p. 308).

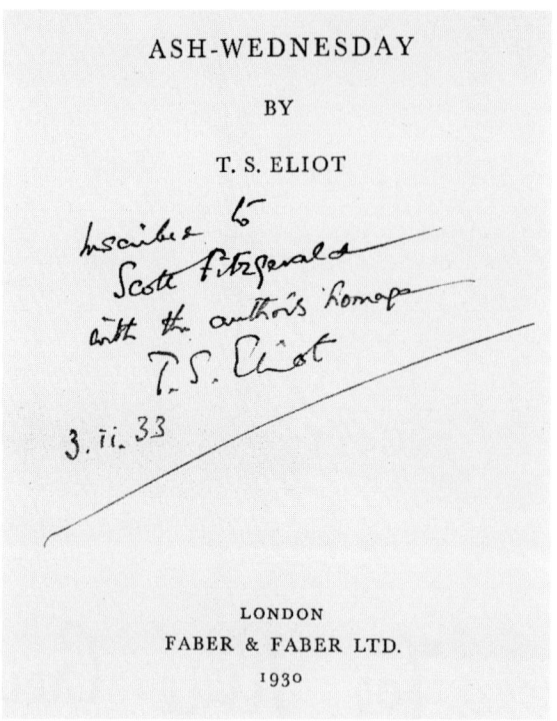

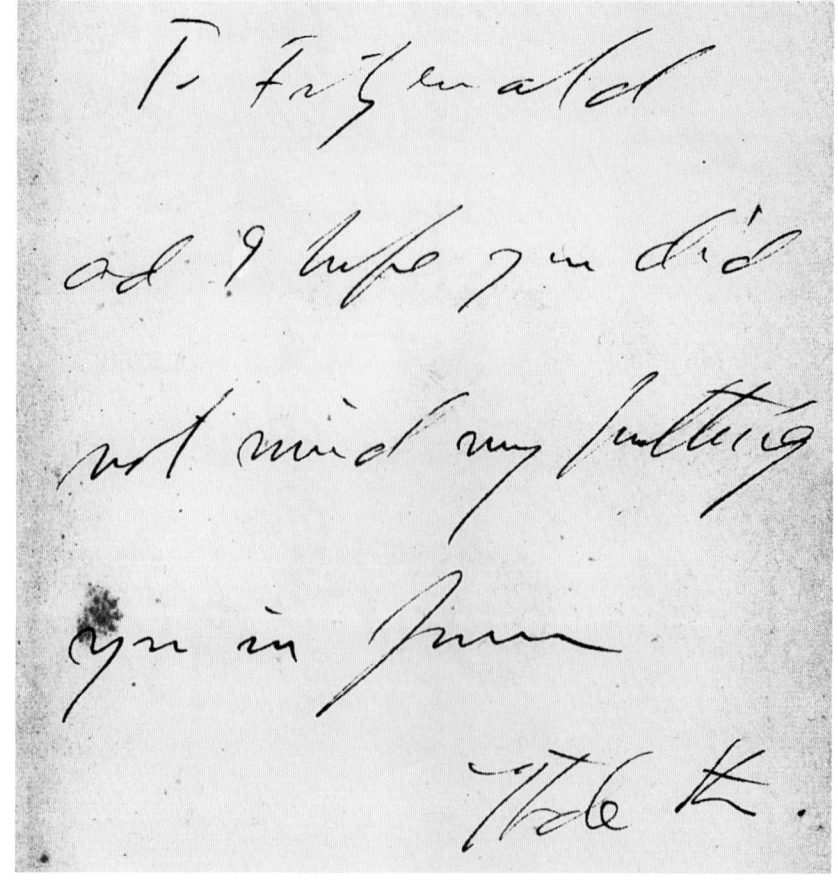

78. Edmund Wilson, *This Room and This Gin and These Sandwiches: Three Plays* (New York: New Republic, 1937): Fitzgerald's copy with holograph annotations.

The note on page 75 indicates that Wilson incorporated Fitzgerald's material for *The Great Gatsby* into the play "The Crime in the Whistler Room." Fitzgerald first met Wilson, who was a year ahead of him, at Princeton, where they worked together on the *Nassau Literary Magazine*. He remained a close friend and adviser throughout Fitzgerald's lifetime, providing, as Fitzgerald put it, "my intellectual conscience." After Fitzgerald's death Wilson edited the unfinished novel *The Last Tycoon* and the collection *The Crack-Up*.

79. Fitzgerald to Cyril Clemens, 1935, TLS, 1 p.

Fitzgerald was asked to provide this statement for a 1935 banquet honoring the centenary of Samuel Langhorne Clemens's birth. It shows Fitzgerald's awareness of American literary history and his concern with reevaluating American myths and dreams, a central element in Fitzgerald's fiction.

The Hollywood Years, 1937–1940

by Cy League

In July 1937 F. Scott Fitzgerald went to work in Hollywood with a six-month M-G-M contract worth $1,000 per week. The decent money that this would be now was a small fortune then, and it came at an critical time, for Fitzgerald was deeply in debt. The sale of short stories had always provided most of Fitzgerald's income, but by summer 1937 he was no longer able to sell to his most lucrative market, *The Saturday Evening Post*. The lower payments by less prosperous magazines could not keep pace with Fitzgerald's expenses. His debts when he left for Hollywood totaled about $40,000, $12,000 of which was owed to his literary agent, Harold Ober.

Fitzgerald had made two trips to Hollywood before 1937. In January 1927 he worked for United Artists on an original screenplay, "Lipstick," which was rejected; the movie went unproduced. It was at this time that he met Irving Thalberg, head of production at M-G-M, who would be the source for the hero of Fitzgerald's last, unfinished novel, *The Love of the Last Tycoon*. In November 1931 Thalberg hired Fitzgerald to work for M-G-M on *Red-Headed Woman*. Fitzgerald's screenplay was rejected, and the movie was eventually produced from a screenplay by Anita Loos. In 1927 and 1931 Fitzgerald had found that earning Hollywood's big money involved specialized skills that he did not possess. With his third trip to Hollywood, Fitzgerald hoped to make up for his earlier failures.

Fitzgerald probably reported to the M-G-M lot on Saturday, July 10, 1937, and began his first full week the following Monday. He was well received, especially by the screenwriting community, among whom he had old friends. On July 14, 1937, one such friend, Robert Benchley, invited Fitzgerald to a party for British Hollywood columnist Sheilah Graham. Within a fortnight Fitzgerald and Graham began a love affair that would last the rest of his life. Graham provided a stabilizing influence that helped to minimize the damage done by the drinking that Fitzgerald fell back into when his Hollywood fortunes declined. Without her devoted companionship Fitzgerald almost certainly would not have written as much as he did of *The Love of the Last Tycoon*.

Fitzgerald's first major assignment was to write a screenplay based on Erich Maria Remarque's 1937 anti-Nazi novel, *Three Comrades*. By September 4, 1937, Fitzgerald had submitted two-thirds of a screenplay to producer Joseph Mankiewicz. At the same time, Fitzgerald requested that he be allowed to continue working alone. He was dismayed when E. E. Paramore, an experienced screenwriter, was assigned as his collaborator. Despite poorly defined roles and artistic differences, Fitzgerald and Paramore managed to work through six drafts of *Three Comrades* and on February 1, 1938, submitted their final version, which Mankiewicz revised. Fitzgerald was angered and offended by Mankiewicz's actions, but he no doubt took comfort in the fact that the *Three Comrades* project earned him both an M-G-M contract renewal for $1,250 per week and his only screen credit.

None of Fitzgerald's subsequent work for M-G-M was as successful as the *Three Comrades* project. He worked for producer Hunt Stromberg on "Infidelity," a project that was doomed from the outset by its plot, which dealt with adultery. Stromberg and Fitzgerald were initially confident that they could write a workable script that would be approved by the Breen Office, the movie industry's arbiter of moral standards. They were unsuccessful, and the project was shelved in May 1938. A June 27, 1938, memo from Fitzgerald to Stromberg shows the author still wrestling with the troublesome plot, but no closer to a workable solution.

After Fitzgerald's next assignment, *Marie Antoinette*, was tabled (later to be made from another screenplay), he worked for Stromberg again on *The*

Women, an adaptation of Clare Booth Luce's Broadway play. Fitzgerald collaborated with an old friend and established screenwriter, Donald Ogden Stewart, but M-G-M felt their screenplay did not live up to Luce's original. Fitzgerald and Stewart were replaced by Jane Murfin and Anita Loos. M-G-M then transferred Fitzgerald to *Madam Curie,* on which he collaborated with producer Sidney Franklin. Fitzgerald and Franklin were unable to satisfy Bernard Hyman, who was in charge of the project. Fitzgerald submitted an incomplete screenplay on January 3, 1938, but the project was shelved, to be produced in 1943 from a new screenplay. During his work on *Madam Curie,* M-G-M informed Fitzgerald that his contract would not be renewed. For the remainder of his contract, which officially expired on January 27, 1939, Fitzgerald was loaned to David O. Selznick for *Gone With the Wind.* He worked for about a week on this film, and his contribution to the final version was negligible.

At the end of January 1939 Fitzgerald became a freelance screenwriter. His post-M-G-M film work resulted in nothing for the screen. Fitzgerald collaborated with Budd Schulberg for producer Walter Wanger on *Winter Carnival,* to be set at Dartmouth College, but went on a bender during a location-shooting trip on campus and was fired. After *Winter Carnival,* with no regular salary coming in, Fitzgerald's financial situation grew desperate. A May 29, 1939, letter to Ober shows Fitzgerald feeling out the short-story market, which he had more or less ignored since coming to Hollywood. Fitzgerald's plans and the guarded optimism he evinces in this letter fail to take into account the fact that his short-story skills had decayed and that the literary marketplace had changed since the Twenties. Only *Esquire* remained a reliable buyer for Fitzgerald's short fiction.

Through fall 1939 and to the end of his life, there were a few brief film assignments, but none of significance, monetary or otherwise. Of the short fiction that Fitzgerald published at this time, the Pat Hobby stories are the most important. Pat Hobby was a fictitious, amoral studio hack about whom Fitzgerald wrote seventeen short sketches for *Esquire.* The Pat Hobby stories have little value as literature; their primary importance is that they earned money that went toward work on a project of undeniable literary value, *The Love of the Last Tycoon.*

By spring 1939 Fitzgerald was planning a novel about Hollywood. He was dissatisfied with other portrayals of the industry and felt that by drawing on his own experience he could create something better. Fitzgerald projected a novel of around 50,000 words—as tightly constructed as *Gatsby*—in which each part would "contribute to the dramatic movement" of the whole. Fitzgerald's work on *Tycoon* made him happy. He was creating serious art again, and he was further inspired by the sense, expressed in an earlier letter to his wife, that this would be his last novel because "[a]fter fifty one is different. One can't remember emotionally. . . ."

Intermittent studio work and the Pat Hobby stories were insufficient to support work on *Tycoon.* In March 1940 Fitzgerald sold the film rights to his short story "Babylon Revisited" (*Post,* February 21, 1931) to independent producer Lester Cowan and agreed to adapt it into a screenplay. Fitzgerald's work for Cowan bought approximately $6,000 worth of writing time for *Tycoon.* Though it was only a little more than half finished (drafts for seventeen of thirty planned episodes) when Fitzgerald died on December 21, 1940, *The Love of the Last Tycoon* contains contains passages of extraordinary depth and beauty.

◆ ◆ ◆

80. Fitzgerald to Anne Ober, July 25, 1937, Hollywood, Calif., ALS, 2 pp.

Fitzgerald wrote to Anne Ober, wife of his literary agent, to make the point that he would rather have serious screenwriting work than be known as a serious fiction writer working in Hollywood. His consternation at the alleged bad conduct of his daughter, Scottie, is also significant. During Fitzgerald's tenure in Hollywood, Scottie stayed with the Obers while on vacation from school, but the author was careful not to neglect his duties as a father. His relations with Anne Ober were often strained by his efforts to father from a distance.

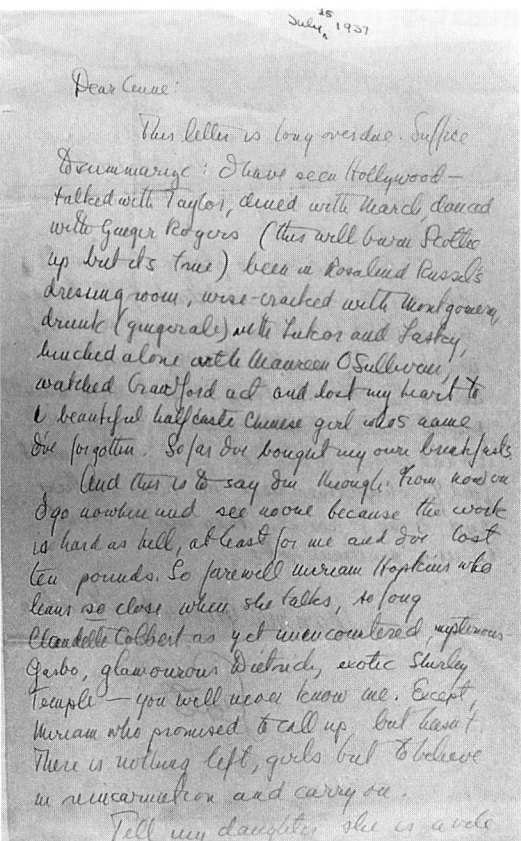

81. Script for *A Yank at Oxford* (M-G-M, 1937)

Fitzgerald's first job under his 1937 contract with M-G-M was to polish the screenplay for *A Yank at Oxford*. Fitzgerald's reputation as a writer of collegiate fiction may have prompted this assignment. The *Yank* project presaged many of the problems that were to plague Fitzgerald's attempt at a screenwriting career. He hated the standard M-G-M practice, originated by Irving Thalberg, of having relays of writers work on single projects. Fitzgerald feared a reprise of an earlier Hollywood experience (his work on *Red-Headed Woman* in 1931) during which, he felt, hostile collaboration had ruined good work and cost him a screen credit. Fitzgerald had emphasized his antipathy toward collaboration, as well as his strategy for circumventing M-G-M's reliance on it, in a July 1937 letter to Scottie:

> I must be very tactful but keep my hand on the wheel from the start—find out the key man among the bosses + the most malleable among the collaborators—then fight the rest tooth + nail until, in fact or in effect, I'm alone on the picture. That's the only way I can do my best work. Given a break I can make them double this contract in less than two years. (*Life in Letters*, p. 331)

82. Script for *Three Comrades* (M-G-M, 1938)

From September 1937 until January 1938 Fitzgerald worked for producer Joseph Mankiewicz on adapting Erich Maria Remarque's 1937 anti-Nazi novel *Three Comrades* to the screen. Mankiewicz substantially revised the final version of the *Three Comrades* screenplay submitted by Fitzgerald and E. E. Paramore. Fitzgerald was offended by these revisions, feeling that his art had been replaced with Hollywood sentimentality. Mankiewicz defended his actions by claiming that Fitzgerald wrote novelistic dialogue that would not work on screen.

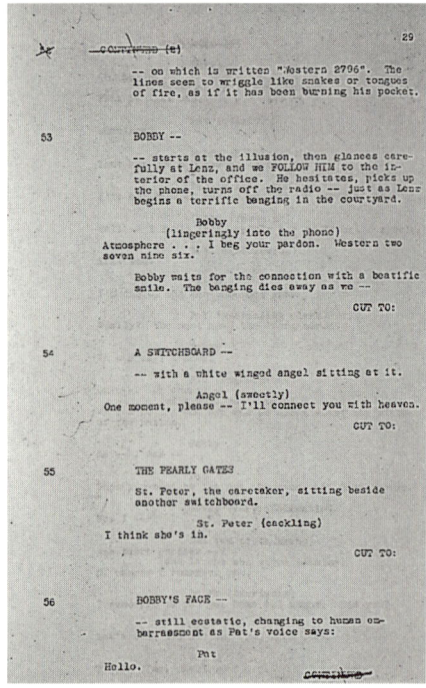

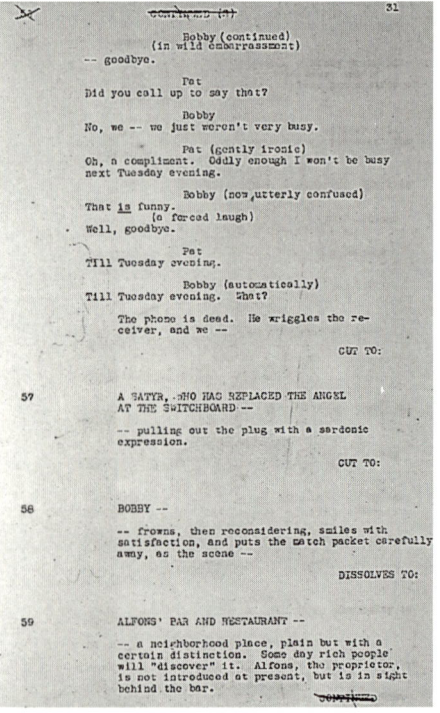

83. Fitzgerald to John Biggs, fall 1937, Hollywood, Calif., ALS, 3 pp.

Fitzgerald wrote this letter to Princeton friend John Biggs while still in the early phase of his tenure in Hollywood, having just finished work on *Three Comrades*. Fitzgerald mentions in passing his collaborator on that project, E. E. Paramore. He also alludes "confidentially" to his salary at M-G-M and the schedule by which it was to increase. Fitzgerald received the raise to $1,250 per week in January 1938, but M-G-M declined to grant him the contract renewal in January 1939 that would have required the studio to raise his salary to $1,500 per week.

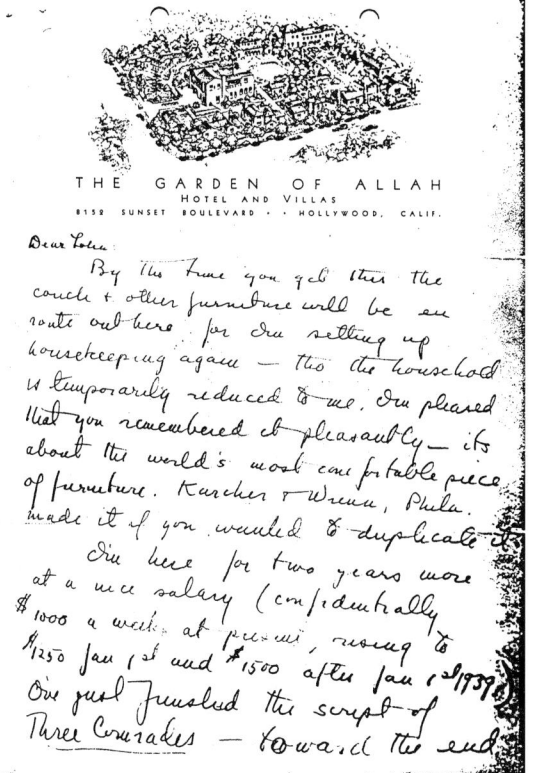

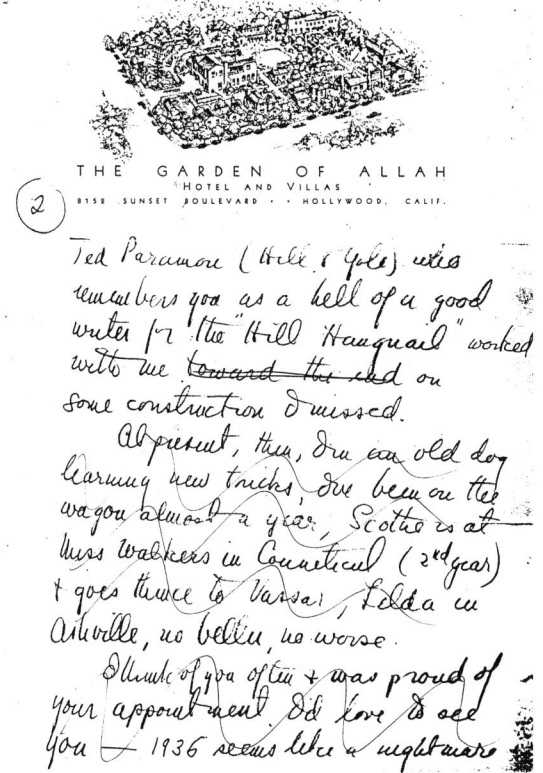

84. Drafts of scripts for M-G-M's "Infidelity" project, 1938; memo to producer Hunt Stromberg, June 27, 1938, CC, 5 pp.

After *Three Comrades*, Fitzgerald was to work without a collaborator on the Hunt Stromberg production, "Infidelity," which was to be a vehicle for Joan Crawford. Stromberg was known as a writer's producer and seems to have left Fitzgerald alone to fashion a workable screenplay. "Infidelity" was crippled from the beginning by the fact that its plot was antithetical to the prevailing cinematic mores of the Thirties. The subject of marital infidelity was deemed a morally unfit subject for film. Fitzgerald tried to give his screenplay a positive moral theme and to move the fictive marriage toward eventual reunion, but he could not tell the story so as to satisfy the Breen Office. Because even the title, "Infidelity," was problematic, producer and writer at one point hit on the desperate expedient of changing the title to "Fidelity." This strategy failed as did all their efforts to create a usable script, and Stromberg eventually scrapped the project in May 1938. A memo from Fitzgerald to Stromberg dated June 27, 1938, shows the author still wrestling with the problematic plot but no closer to a workable solution. His latest proposed version of the film has two acts of infidelity, one divorce, and no chance of a comfortable ending; such a screenplay had little chance of being produced. "Infidelity" was published in *Esquire* in December 1973.

```
                                    INFIDELITY
                                    From: F. Scott Fitzgerald
                                    June 27, 1938

Dear Hunt:

        For a month I have been thinking about INFIDELITY,
inventing and rejecting solutions. I have arrived at some
clear thinking about it and the chief difficulty has been how
to present it to you. Perhaps the best way is to tell it to
you exactly as it came to me, so while Sidney is in the
hospital, I'm stealing this day from THE WOMEN, to do just
that.

        In the first place, I have been stymied all through
by my mental picture of the casting. It isn't my business,
but such conceptions are not easy to get out of one's mind:

        Instead of seeing our heroine Althea pursued by
two attractive men, Gable and Cooper, as you suggested, I kept
seeing Joan Crawford between Gable and Tone — between a star
and a leading man. It was a dull thought. It was hard to
tell the story, knowing that the audience was thinking ahead
of you.

        To clear my mind I have assumed a new cast of
characters. For the sake of the picture, let me imagine that
Althea is Myrna Loy, Nicolas is Clark Gable, and Alex, her
old sweetheart, is Robert Taylor. Immediately the whole
thing brightened for me. I could imagine Myrna Loy loving
either one of them, I could imagine either one of them losing
her without making the picture ridiculous. And I could
imagine an exciting doubt up to the very end as to which one
was going to win. For there is no question about it — this
is a Three Star Picture.
```

85. Fitzgerald to Anne Ober, March 4, 1938, Hollywood, Calif., TLS, 3 pp.

Fitzgerald's letter to Anne Ober displays his long-range interest in Scottie's welfare as he critiques her alleged interest in attending Bryn Mawr after leaving the Walker School (she eventually attended Vassar). He tries here, as in many of his letters to and about his daughter, to prevent her from taking college as lightly as he himself had done. Later in the letter Fitzgerald mentions the recently completed *Three Comrades* project, expresses his bitterness over script changes Joseph Mankiewicz had made, and incorrectly predicts box-office failure for the film. The letter's conclusion shows his growing disillusionment with Hollywood and the film industry.

86. Fitzgerald to Anne and Harold Ober, March 11, 1938, Hollywood, Calif., TLS, 1 p.

Fitzgerald's March 11, 1938, letter to the Obers opens with concern for Scottie's welfare. The importance of the Obers to Scottie at this time is clearly demonstrated. They were in essence her surrogate parents. At the end of this short letter, Fitzgerald mentions "Infidelity," the project that he worked on for M-G-M after *Three Comrades*.

THE GARDEN OF ALLAH
HOTEL AND VILLAS
8152 SUNSET BOULEVARD · · HOLLYWOOD, CALIF.
CABLE ADDRESS—GARDALLAH

March 11th, 1938

Dear Anne and Harold:

    It was perfectly magnificent of you to go up to Scottie's play. Thank you for the report on her success, and most sincere sympathy for having to sit next to the headmistress. Harold, I'll bet you writhed and expected at any moment to be kept after school -- I know I should have. There is something about that atmosphere from which a child never really recovers.

    I am a third through "Infidelity" -- Crawford picture. I suspect that Hunt Stromberg is going to put the pressure on, but he isn't going to succeed. I worked myself half sick on the last picture and I am going to keep to a safe and sane schedule on this one. Also, I'am not going to be kept here Easter. I'm awfully glad now that I wrote the vacations into my contract. Again, a thousand thanks.

Scott

Mr. and Mrs. Harold Ober
Dromore Road
Scarsdale, New York

87. Fitzgerald to Zelda Fitzgerald, c. April 1938, Hollywood, Calif., ALS, 2 pp.

When this perhaps unmailed letter was written, Fitzgerald was near the end of his time on the unsuccessful "Infidelity" project. He had recently returned from a disastrous vacation with Scottie and Zelda, and the letter is largely an effort to come to an understanding with his wife. Fitzgerald also shows his understanding of the importance of the screen credit he earned on the *Three Comrades* project and his awareness of the need another such credit to solidify his position in Hollywood.

I couldn't bring myself to write you last week — I was plenty sore with myself and also a good deal with you. But as things settle down I can regard it all with some detachment. As I told you I was a sick man when I left California — had a beautiful little hemorage the end of March, the first in two years and a half — and I was carrying on only on the false exaltation of having done some really excellent work. I thought I'd just lie around in Norfolk and rest but it was a fantastic idea because I should have rested before undertaking the trip. There has been no drink out here, not a drop of it, but I am in an unfortunate rut of caffene by day and chloral by night which is about as bad on the nerves. As I told you if I can finish one excellent picture to top Three Comrades I think I can bargain for better terms — more rest and more money.

These are a lot of "I"s to tell you I worry about you — my condition must have been a strain and I thought you had developed somewhat grandiose ideas of how to spend this money, I am to spring which I consider as capital — this extravagant trip to the contrary. Dr. Carrol's feeling about money is simply that he wants to regulate your affairs for the time being and he can do so (over)

88. *Madame Curie* scripts (M-G-M, 1938–1939).

The last M-G-M project on which Fitzgerald did significant work was *Madame Curie* (November 1938 to January 1939). M-G-M had for some time before November 1938 been trying to come up with an adequate screenplay depiction of the Curies' lives. Aldous Huxley had worked with little success on the project, and Fitzgerald was called in shortly after Huxley's script was rejected. Fitzgerald and producer Sidney Franklin collaborated on the difficult task of balancing the necessary love plot with accurate biography in a manner that would please Bernard Hyman, head of the production unit in charge of the film. Hyman saw the film as essentially a love story and rejected Fitzgerald and Franklin's various proposals, presumably because they were too serious and too much stressed the Curies' scientific achievements. Fitzgerald submitted an incomplete screenplay on January 3, 1939, but Hyman had seen enough; the project was shelved. During his work on *Madame Curie*, Fitzgerald was informed by Hyman at a Christmas party that his M-G-M contract would not be renewed.

89. Fitzgerald's 1938 tax returns.

In 1938, Fitzgerald's only calendar year under contract to M-G-M, he earned $58,783.10. Under California law Fitzgerald could assign half of his income to his wife. This allowed him to pay taxes in a lower bracket.

90. H. N. Swanson to Fitzgerald, January 21, 1939, Hollywood, Calif., TLS, 1 p.

This letter from Fitzgerald's first Hollywood agent answers a question that the author had about M-G-M's administration of his 1938 contract. The studio had exercised its option to extend Fitzgerald's contract until January 27 to make up for time he had taken off earlier in the year. Swanson also clarifies the terms of Fitzgerald's work for David O. Selznick on *Gone With the Wind*.

91. Contract with the Phil Berg–Bert Allenberg agency, signed by Fitzgerald, February 22, 1940.

In February 1940 Fitzgerald retained the Phil Berg–Bert Allenberg agency to find employment for him as a screenwriter. Dissatisfied with his screenwriting career, Fitzgerald replaced H. N. Swanson with Leland Heyward, but when his Hollywood fortunes did not improve, he finally switched to the Berg-Allenberg agency. Fitzgerald blamed his agents in part for the state of his screenwriting career, but the fault lay rather with the nature of the movie business and of his own talent.

92. Contract with Lester Cowan for the "Babylon Revisited" screenplay, April 8, 1940.

By April 1939 Fitzgerald had been working for about a year on *The Love of the Last Tycoon*. Money was scarce during that period in that freelance studio work was sporadic, and the Pat Hobby stories brought in only $250 each. In April 1940 Fitzgerald sold the rights to his short story "Babylon Revisited" to independent movie producer Lester Cowan for $1,000 and agreed to work for $500 per week on turning it into a screenplay. In all Fitzgerald received around $6,000 from Cowan, money which contributed substantially toward work on *Tycoon*. Fitzgerald's screenplay, renamed "Cosmopolitan," is a loose adaptation of the original (see item 57). Fitzgerald expanded the role of the child in the short story and changed her name to Victoria. The project collapsed when Cowan and Fitzgerald were unable to secure Shirley Temple for the lead role. "Cosmopolitan" has the reputation of being Fitzgerald's best screenplay, but such a claim is difficult to test because it was never filmed—though it was published in 1993. Fitzgerald avails himself of many of the sentimental plot contrivances that he had earlier decried (e.g., during the *Three Comrades* project), but he may have been trying to write a Hollywood-style screenplay.

93. Fitzgerald to Alice Wooton, July 29, 1940, Santa Barbara, Calif., TLS, 1 p.

Alice Wooton worked as Fitzgerald's secretary in Baltimore during the time that he was composing the Philippe short stories. In this postscript to a friendly letter Fitzgerald displays his bitterness and disillusionment about Hollywood, brought on by the failure of his screenwriting career, by his inability to get sufficient backing for *The Love of the Last Tycoon*, and by his financial situation in general.

```
                Santa Barbara, California



      P.S.   Isn't Hollywood a dump--in the human sense of the word.
             A hideous town, pointed up by the insulting gardens of
             its rich, full of the human spirit at a new low of debase-
             ment.
```

94. Fitzgerald's notebook, c. 1938–1940, 4 3/4" x 6", 6 pp. with holograph entries.

During the time that Fitzgerald was working on *The Love of the Last Tycoon*, he kept a reporter's notebook in which to record thoughts and observations that might make their way into the novel. On the first page of what remains of this notebook (pages are missing), Fitzgerald describes Hollywood types whom he has encountered and distinguishes them from Monroe Stahr, the hero of *The Love of the Last Tycoon*.

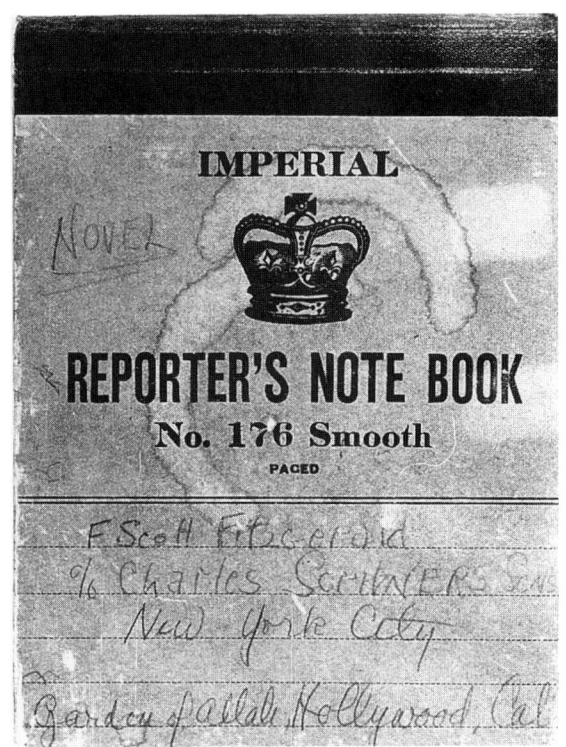

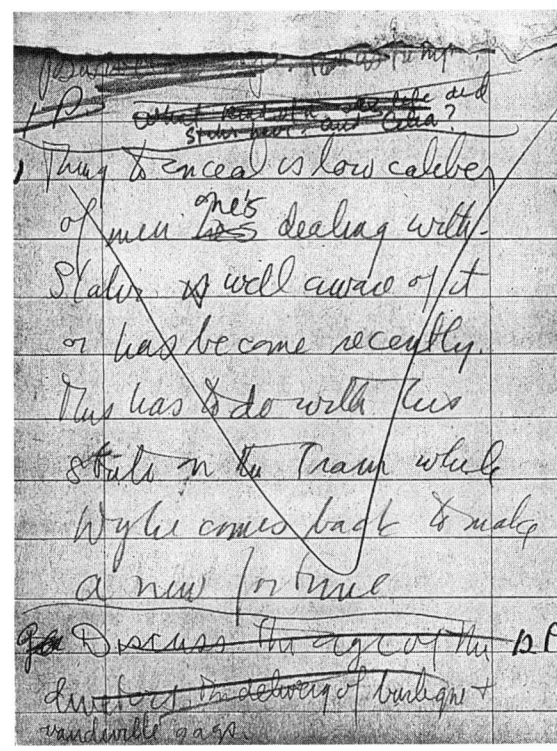

Second Act
Resurrection and Restoration

by Catherine E. Lewis

In "Notes About My Now-Famous Father," Scottie Fitzgerald Smith, daughter of F. Scott Fitzgerald, states that 1974 marked the twenty-fifth anniversary of the first time someone asked her why she "thought [her] father's writings were having such a revival" (p. 118). Twenty-five years prior to Smith's article would have been 1949, the year that falls roughly in the middle of the twenty years during which Fitzgerald's reputation was resurrected. The success of Fitzgerald's works since then demonstrates that the revival solidified into canonized reputation.

When Fitzgerald died on December 21, 1940, he was aware that his salability had diminished even though nine of his titles were available from Scribners. In a May 20, 1940, letter to Maxwell Perkins, his editor at Scribners, Fitzgerald laments his market decline:

> I wish I was in print. It will be odd a year or so from now when Scottie assures her friends I was an author and finds that no book is procurable. . . . Would the 25 cent press keep *Gatsby* in the public eye—or *is the book unpopular*. Has it *had* its chance? Would a popular reissue in that series with a preface *not* by me but by one of its admirers—I can maybe pick one—make it a favorite with class rooms, profs, lovers of English prose—anybody. (*Life in Letters*, p. 445)

Copies of his novels and short-story collections were not selling; his last royalty check from Scribners was $13.13.

Just as no one reason explains the decline of Fitzgerald's reputation, then no single reason accounts for the resurgence of interest. Post-war nostalgia, Fitzgerald's early death, and the expansion of new media have all been offered as possible reasons why both scholarly and popular interest in Fitzgerald's work increased markedly. From the year of his death throughout the next two decades Fitzgerald's popularity and place in the literary market far exceeded the being "in print" he hoped for in the letter to Perkins. Part of what sparked the interest was that the man who had known newspaper celebrity in his youth had virtually disappeared from the pages of magazines. Thus, when his name appeared again at the time of his death, interest in him regenerated because of the sensational appeal of the early death and his reduced circumstances and because of the Hollywood lure of his work in progress, to be titled *The Love of the Last Tycoon: A Western*. But such superficial attention gave way to the stronger, specific publishing events that were the impetuses for what would soon be called the "Fitzgerald revival."

At the time of Fitzgerald's death Perkins decided to publish *The Last Tycoon* as it was, but he realized that the buying public would be more likely to buy a collection of Fitzgerald's work than a single, unfinished novel. He decided to include *The Great Gatsby* and a selection of Fitzgerald's stories along with *The Last Tycoon* in an omnibus collection edited by Fitzgerald's college friend, the influential literary critic Edmund Wilson. Furthermore Wilson assembled a series of obituary-tributes in the February and March 1941 issues of *The New Republic* by authors who had known Fitzgerald and respected his work: John Dos Passos, John Peale Bishop, John O'Hara, Glenway Wescott, and Budd Schulberg.

The year 1945 offered evidence that Fitzgerald's posthumous career was strengthening. With the publication of *The Crack-Up* in 1945, Wilson further stimulated interest in Fitzgerald. This collection of autobiographical essays by Fitzgerald and letters and tributes to him from other authors provides insight into Fitzgerald as a writer and as a man of literary intelligence and depth. The next notable event was the publication of *The Portable F. Scott Fitzgerald* by Viking Press. Again Fitzgerald's literary friends were vital in promoting him, for the volume's contents were selected by Dorothy Parker and introduced by John O'Hara. This collection includes *The Great Gatsby, Tender Is the Night,* and nine stories. O'Hara's preface is full of admiration: "All he was was our best novelist, one of our best novella-ists, and one of our finest writers of short stories" (xiv). A high point of the Fitzgerald activity of 1945 was the publication of two volumes, *The Great Gatsby* and *The Diamond as Big as the Ritz and Other Stories,* in the Armed Services Editions, which provided more than 150,000 copies of Fitzgerald's works for distribution to the servicemen. The popular market was also receptive to the publication of Fitzgerald's works in the 1940s. The most significant event was the decision by Bantam in 1946 to print *The Great Gatsby* as one of its first ten titles when the company entered into the book market with paperbound editions.

Fitzgerald was also marketed to a mass audience by means of motion-picture, radio, and television adaptations. In 1949 *The Great Gatsby* was produced as a film starring Alan Ladd. When the film was released the publishing and film worlds intersected, for Grosset and Dunlap added a band to its *Gatsby* to announce the film, and Bantam added a dust jacket to the cover of its paperback *Gatsby* that showed a picture of Ladd.

The next period of the Fitzgerald revival was the early 1950s, and the number of serious evaluations of Fitzgerald's work increased. Scottie Fitzgerald donated her father's papers to the Princeton University Library in 1950, and the gift stimulated scholarly interest in Fitzgerald. Arthur Mizener published the first book-length Fitzgerald biography, *The Far Side of Paradise,* in January 1951. Scribners published a new collection of Fitzgerald's short stories that was edited by critic Malcolm Cowley. Later that year Cowley published *Tender Is the Night* with what Fitzgerald had declared were his final revisions to the novel.

Budd Schulberg fed the popular interest with a novel based on Fitzgerald in Hollywood, *The Disenchanted* (1950). The increase in sales that came with paperback printings of Fitzgerald works was worldwide. In England, Penguin published and distributed Fitzgerald's titles in paperback and kept his name before the broad British market. *The Great Gatsby* (1950) was the first of the novels published by Penguin; *Tender Is the Night* (the revised version) was added to the line in 1954, and *The Last Tycoon* appeared in 1960. Television, too, gave attention to Fitzgerald, for adaptations of his novels, and short stories were broadcast in the late 1940s and throughout the 1950s: *The Last Tycoon* (1949), "The Rich Boy" (1952), and *The Great Gatsby* (1958) were produced for the Philco Television Playhouse series. *The Last Tycoon* (1951) and *The Great Gatsby* (1955) were part of *Robert Montgomery Presents* and also aired on CBS's *Playhouse 90* (*The Last Tycoon* in 1957 and *The Great Gatsby* in 1958). DuMont Television produced "Babylon Revisited" for broadcast in 1953.

Since his death on December 21, 1940, F. Scott Fitzgerald's writings have been given more attention than they had during his lifetime. Fitzgerald died too early to see that academic attention, paperbound editions, and increased markets for subsidiary rights would eventually help to establish him permanently in the American and worldwide literary canons. In one of the last lines of the "HOLLYWOOD, ETC" section of the notes to *The Love of the Last Tycoon,* F. Scott Fitzgerald wrote, "There are no second acts in American lives" (p. 163). To Fitzgerald's dismay what he regarded as the only act of his writing career closed with attention to his writing at its ebb. But in contradiction to his own statement there has been a second act—one that has grown into a separate drama.

◆ ◆ ◆

95. Fitzgerald to Rosalind Sayre Smith, March 4, 1938, Hollywood, Calif., TLS, 1 p.

Fitzgerald responds to a question Smith, his sister-in-law, had apparently asked about a first printing of *The Great Gatsby*. Fitzgerald mentions that Scribners still had copies of the second printing of *The Great Gatsby* in stock at the time of this letter, for his books were not selling. The comment in the letter that Scribners sold copies to Modern Library is incorrect: that firm had published its own printing of *The Great Gatsby* (1934).

```
                              Garden of Allah
                              8152 Sunset Boulevard
                              Hollywood, California

                              March 4th, 1938


        Mrs. Newman Smith
        44 Gramercy Park
        New York City

        Dear Rosalind:
                    I don't think a first edition
        of "The Great Gatsby" is marked any differ-
        ently from any other edition. As I remember,
        they printed 20,000 and then 10,000 more
        when it looked as if it was going to sell,
        and they still have most of that in stock
        except 5,000 copies which they sold to the
        Modern Library.
                    I am having a copy of "Tales
        of the Jazz Age" sent you from Scribner's.
        Wish I could autograph it for you.
                    Zelda is looking forward to
        her sortie from the hospital.

                                   Ever,

                                   Scott

        P.S. Hope you are feeling much better.
```

96. *The Great Gatsby* (New York: Modern Library, 1934).

The Modern Library publication of *The Great Gatsby* went through one printing only, probably in a run of 5,000 copies; it was the fourth printing of the novel. A new introduction by Fitzgerald was included in this printing. The copies sold for 95¢, but sales were insufficient for Modern Library to keep the novel in print. 'DISCONTINUED TITLE' is stamped across the jacket of some copies of the book. The negligible sales of Fitzgerald's books in the 1930s made the later Fitzgerald revival a notable one in American letters.

87

97. Sheilah Graham to Cecilia Delihant Taylor, January 9, 1941, Hollywood, Calif., TLS, 2 pp.

The letter was written to Cecilia "Ceci" Taylor, F. Scott Fitzgerald's cousin, approximately three weeks after Fitzgerald's death (see item 161). The last paragraph is of particular interest because Graham writes of Maxwell Perkins's plan to issue a "memorial book that will include extracts from the new book and perhaps 'The Great Gatsby' and some of Scott's best short stories." Perkins's intention was realized when Scribners published later that year the collection Graham mentions.

1443 North Hayworth Avenue
Hollywood, California
January 9, 1941

Dear Mrs. Taylor:

Your letter only arrived this morning - Thursday. It must have been delayed in the mails because of the Holiday rush.

It is a little hard for me to talk about Scott's death. It was such a tremendous shock, and I still find it impossible to believe. But here are some things that will please you. For the past year he had been quite happy. Everything seemed to be going so well for him. Zelda was much better. Scottie was pleasing him enormously with her letters and her emergence as a writer. And above all, he was working on a new novel and working well. The day before he died, he had mastered one of the most difficult sections of his book, and his joy and radiance will stay with me as long as I live.

As you know, his health had not been good for years, and in Hollywood he lived a very quiet life. (This, too, will please you. There was no liquor for the past year and a month, and there never would have been again.)

About a year ago he complained of pains in his arms, and I think a cardiogram was taken of his heart then, but showed nothing. About six weeks ago, he keeled over after walking to a drug store on the corner of the street in which he lived. His doctor took another cardiogram of his heart, and this time found something wrong. But he said it was of no major seriousness, and that Scott should just refrain from much activity, not to climb stairs or lift anything, and to stay as close to his bed as possible, which Scott did. Two weeks after his first cardiogram was taken, the doctor took another, and this showed such definite improvement that Scott became a fraction more active - but not much.

On the day that he died, the doctor was coming to take another cardiogram, which we were hopefully sure would say that he was better still. Scott and I had lunch together. He wanted to go to the drug store for an ice cream cone, but decided he would wait for the doctor's visit. He was laughing and joking, and seemed quite happy. He was reading a book and suddenly jerked to his feet and fell down and died immediately. There was no priest present with him. He was dead before the doctors arrived and tried to revive him with a pulmotor machine, but he died instantaneously

Page 2.

without any knowledge - and without any pain. He died the way I know he would have preferred to die - without a long, lingering, painful illness. And for that, I am very glad. I immediately contacted Scottie and one of the executors of his will, who took charge of all arrangements.

You were one of the few of his relatives that he talked about with me. He was utterly fond of you and told me a great deal about your courage and your beauty.

It is just too sad that he died before he could finish his book. But there may be some salvage, and Max Perkins of Scribners is planning some form of memorial book that will include extracts from the new book and perhaps "The Great Gatsby" and some of Scott's best short stories. And there will also be forewords by prominent writers of today who appreciated Scott's fine prose.

Sheilah Graham

98. *The Last Tycoon: An Unfinished Novel, Together with The Great Gatsby, and Selected Short Stories* (New York: Scribners, 1941), review copy with review slip laid in.

Perkins decided at the time of Fitzgerald's death to publish the draft and notes for Fitzgerald's novel in progress, along with *The Great Gatsby* and five of Fitzgerald's stories to add to the marketability of the unfinished novel. The stories are "May Day," "The Diamond as Big as the Ritz," "The Rich Boy," "Crazy Sunday," and "Absolution." Edmund Wilson was chosen to introduce the volume and select the stories because of his status in the literary world and his longtime association with Fitzgerald. See color insert.

99. *The Crack-Up,* edited by Edmund Wilson (New York: New Directions, 1945).

For this volume Wilson selected stories and nonfiction by Fitzgerald that show him to be an author of literary insight and wit. Included are "Echoes of the Jazz Age," "My Lost City," "Ring," "Show Mr. and Mrs. F to Number ___," "Auction—Model 1934," "Sleeping and Waking," "The Crack-Up," "Handle with Care," "Pasting It Together," and "Early Success," along with selections from Fitzgerald's notebooks and letters. Additionally, Wilson included essays, letters, and tributes by prominent authors, such as Gertrude Stein, Edith Wharton, T. S. Eliot, and Thomas Wolfe. The title of this work is taken from an essay published in *Esquire* in 1936. The book was immediately successful and has not gone out of print since its initial publication.

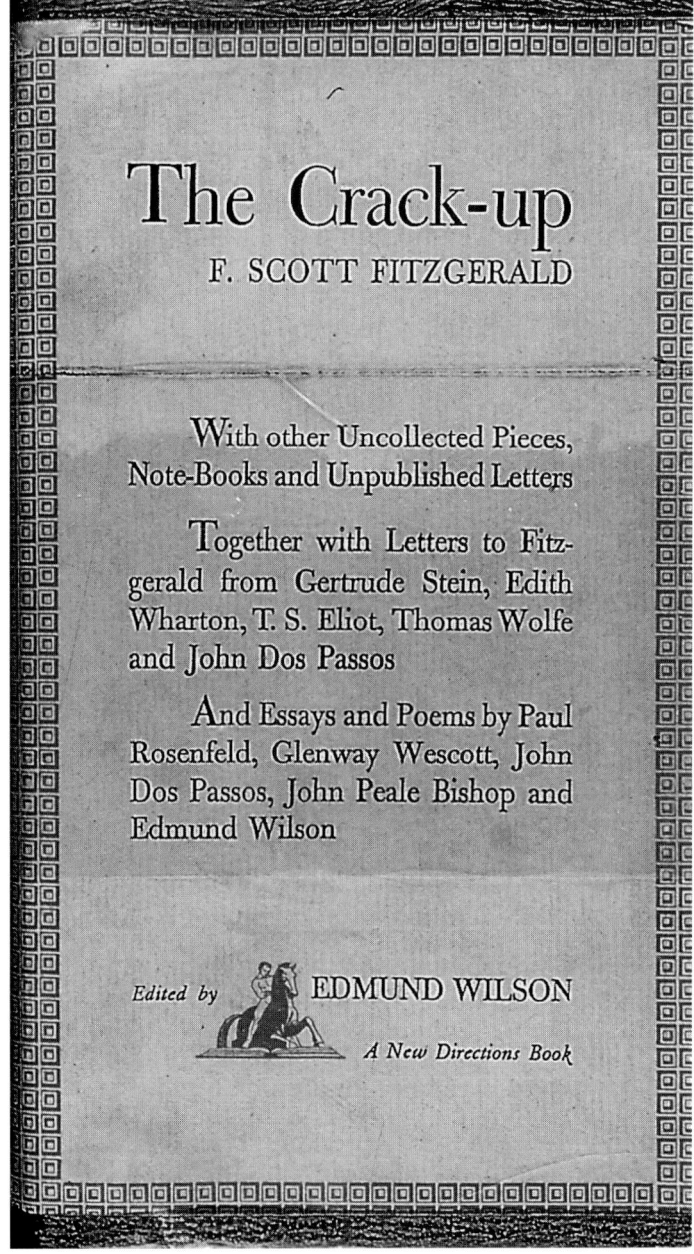

100. *The Portable F. Scott Fitzgerald,* selected by Dorothy Parker, with introduction by John O'Hara (New York: Viking, 1945), Kenneth Millar's copy.

Dorothy Parker had been a longtime friend of Fitzgerald. John O'Hara's introduction is full of exuberance and admiration. The collection includes *The Great Gatsby, Tender Is the Night,* and nine stories. This copy belonged to Kenneth Millar, who wrote under the pseudonym Ross Macdonald. He marked it copiously on the flyleaves and throughout the text. His notes include comments about the God-like eyes of the Dr. T. J. Eckleburg billboard, and he draws a connection between Western success and determination and Gatsby's patron Dan Cody by noting that the name is taken from "Dan'l Boone + Buffalo Bill Cody."

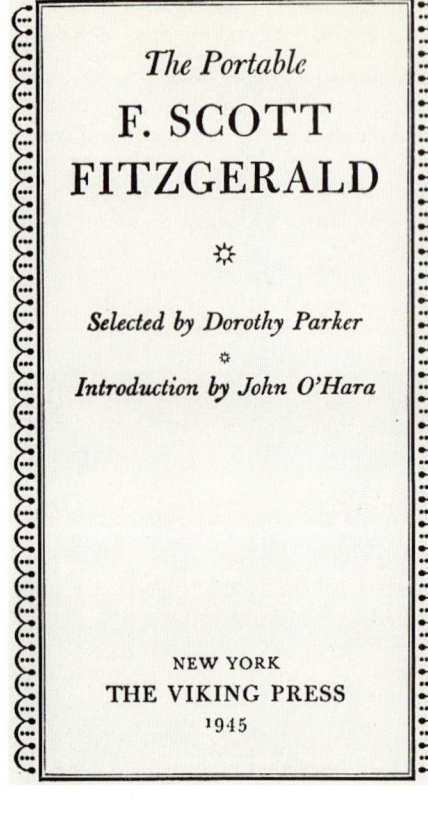
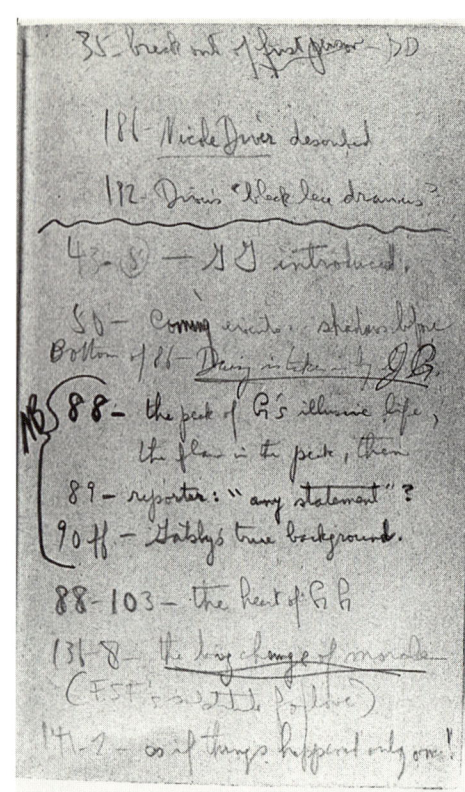
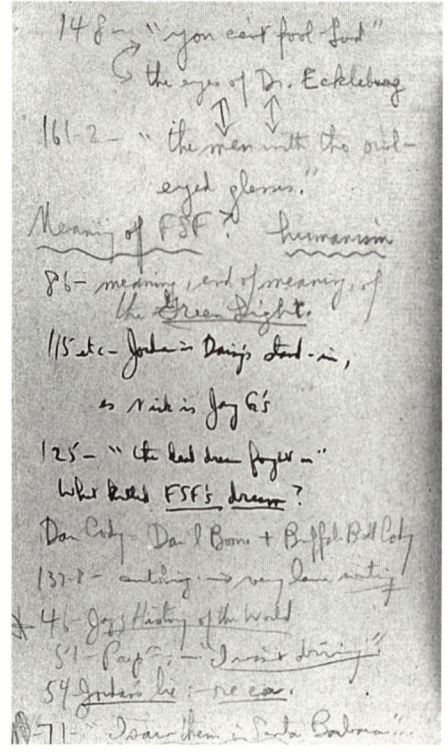
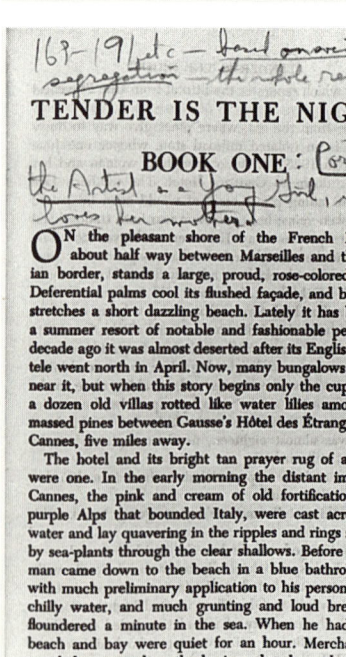

101. *The Great Gatsby,* Armed Services Edition 862 (New York: Council on Books in Wartime, 1945); *The Diamond as Big as the Ritz and Other Stories,* introduction by Louis Untermeyer, Armed Services Editions 1043 (New York: Council on Books in Wartime, 1946).

Armed Services Editions were published for the distribution of small, free copies of books to the troops; 155,000 copies of *The Great Gatsby* and approximately 90,000 copies of *The Diamond as Big as the Ritz and Other Stories* were printed and distributed. Ten stories were included in the collection—among them, "Babylon Revisited," "May Day," "The Rich Boy," and "Winter Dreams"; thus, it was new compilation rather than a reedition of an existing collection. Because of these editions *The Great Gatsby* and several of Fitzgerald's best short stories were made available to a large audience, many of whom would soon enter college classrooms under the GI Bill; consequently Fitzgerald's work was introduced on an extensive basis to a new, more mature generation of readers.

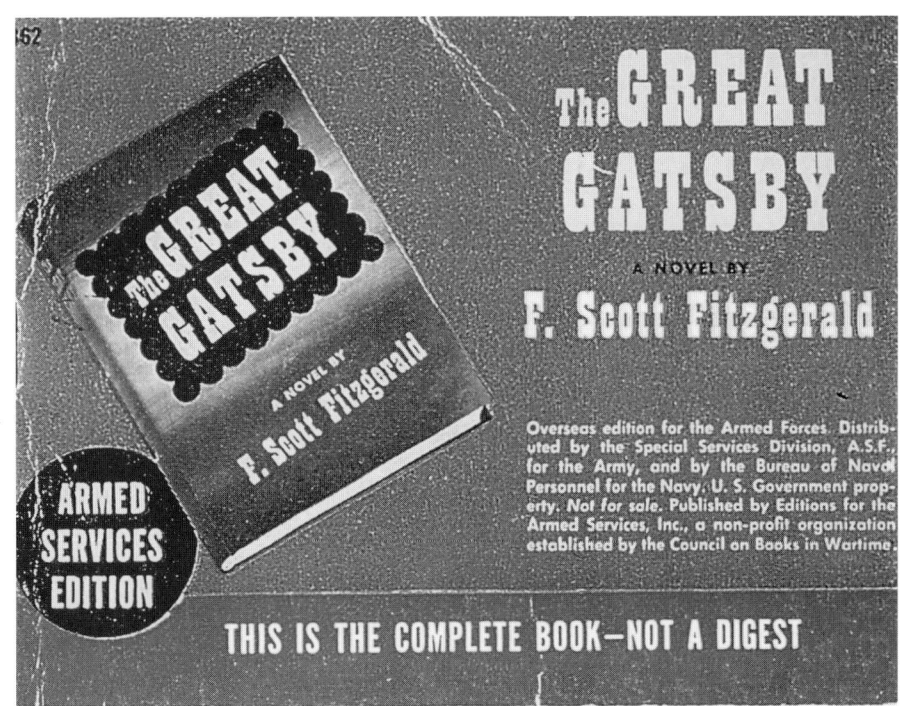

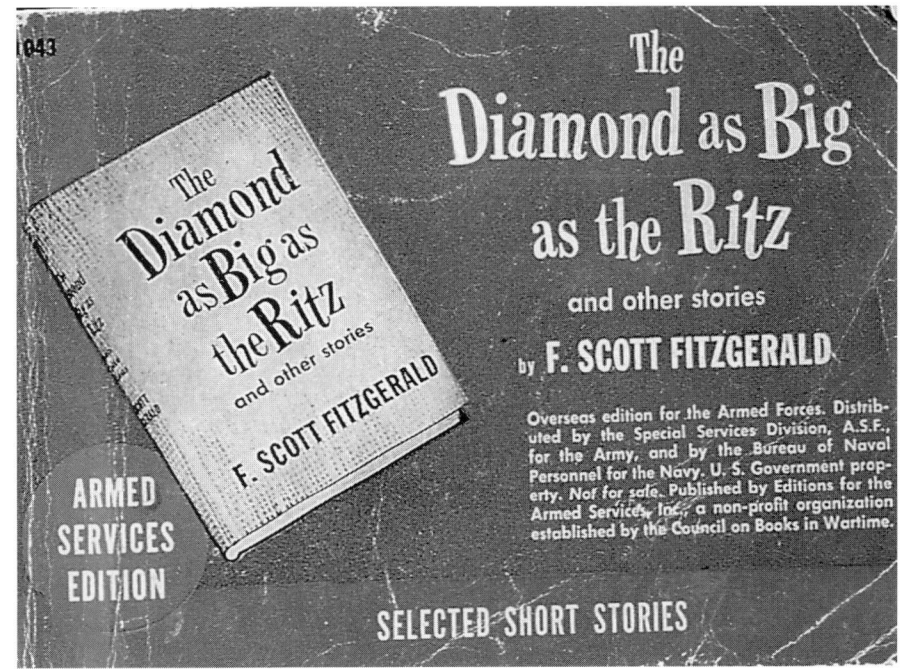

102. *The Great Gatsby* **(New York: Bantam, 1945).**

Number 8 of Bantam's first ten titles, this edition was reprinted twice in 1946, then again in 1951, 1952, and 1954. During the last half of 1951 the Bantam edition sold 140,701 copies (see item 111). The cost of each Bantam paperback was 25¢.

103. *The Great Gatsby* **(New York: Bantam, 1946), second Bantam printing with movie tie-in dust jacket.**

The dust jacket was added to capitalize on the 1949 Paramount Pictures movie starring Alan Ladd.

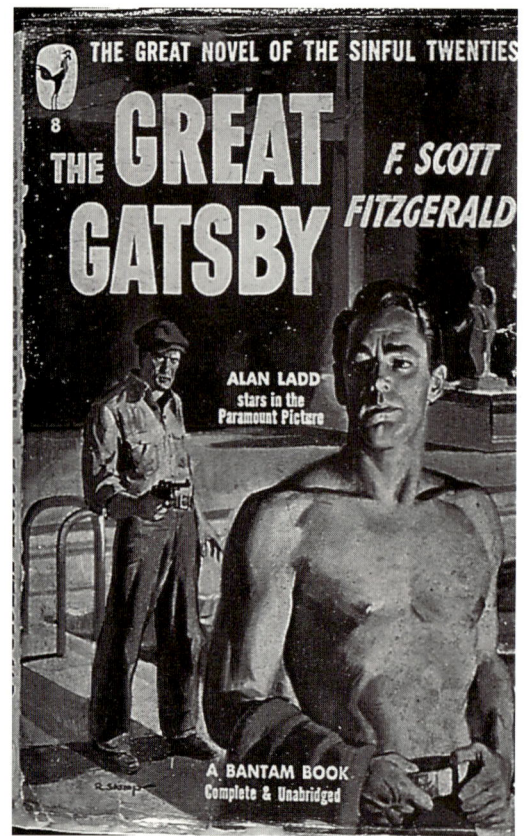

104. Cyril Hume and Richard Maibaum, *The Great Gatsby* screen adaptation (Paramount Pictures), final white script, February 25, 1948.

This production script begins with a scene that has Nick Carraway and Jordan Baker placing flowers on Jay Gatsby's grave, a scene that acts as a framing device for the main story. The film was directed by Elliott Nugent and starred Alan Ladd, Betty Field, Barry Sullivan, Macdonald Carey, Ruth Hussey, Shelley Winters, Howard da Silva, and Ed Begley (see color insert).

105. *The Great Gatsby* (New York: Grosset & Dunlap, 1949).

Grosset & Dunlap leased reprint rights and plates from Scribners in order to produce $1 clothbound copies of the book. A band was added to the book to capitalize on the Paramount Pictures movie starring Alan Ladd.

106. *The Great Gatsby* (New York: Grosset & Dunlap, 1949), Sylvia Plath's copy.

This copy of the novel has Plath's handwritten annotations on thirteen pages; the notes and underlinings were probably made during her undergraduate career at Smith College. Along with her "knight-dragon-princess" note, which reflects her later interest in inverted fairy-tale imagery, Plath also anticipates her future theme of parental neglect. Beside the Daisy-Pammy episode, Plath writes in the margin: "stage property" and "No real relation to the child" (p. 140).

107. *The Stories of F. Scott Fitzgerald*, selected and introduced by Malcolm Cowley (New York: Scribners, 1951), inscribed by Cowley.

A collection of twenty-eight stories. Cowley wrote in the inscription: "Contains eleven previously uncollected stories." Those stories are "Magnetism," "The Rough Crossing," "The Bridal Party," "Two Wrongs," "An Alcoholic Case," "The Long Way Out," "Financing Finnegan," "A Patriotic Short," "Two Old-Timers," "Three Hours Between Planes," and "The Lost Decade."

108. *Tender Is the Night*, "With the author's final revisions and a preface by Malcolm Cowley" (New York: Scribners, 1951).

Cowley used the copy of *Tender* that Fitzgerald had cut and reordered to produce this edition. Fitzgerald had written in his copy, "This is the *final version* of the book as I would like it." This later form of the novel had five books of chapters instead of three. The beginning of the original novel shifts to the middle of the revised one, an effort from Fitzgerald to "correct" the chronology of the novel, a point on which reviewers had criticized the work. The novel then begins with Dick Diver's arrival in Zürich, rather than with Rosemary Hoyt's visit to the Riviera. Changes in spelling, phrasing, and punctuation appear as Fitzgerald revised them. Cowley includes an appendix that discusses the manuscript of *Tender* and notes on the revised text.

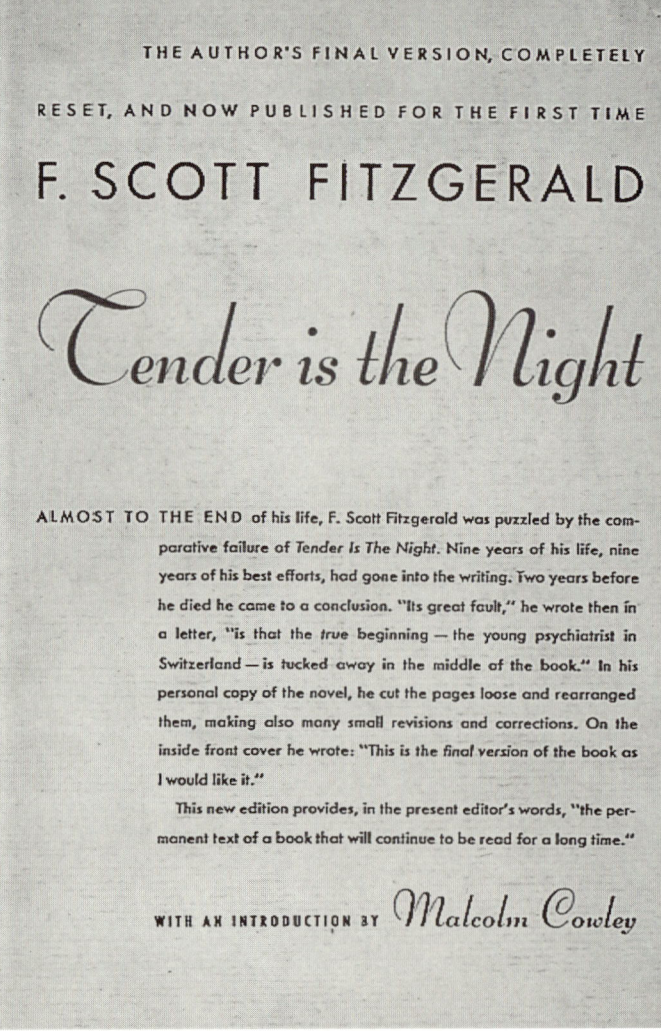

109. *Tender Is the Night* (New York: Bantam, 1951).

This third American edition of the original version of *Tender Is the Night* went through two reprintings in February and April 1951. Sales for this book were substantial; the February 1952 Scribners royalty report shows that Bantam sold 353,600 copies of its *Tender Is the Night* edition during the last half of 1951 (see item 111). This publication, along with Malcolm Cowley's editions of the stories and the "Final Version" of *Tender Is the Night*, establishes 1951 as one of the key years in the Fitzgerald revival.

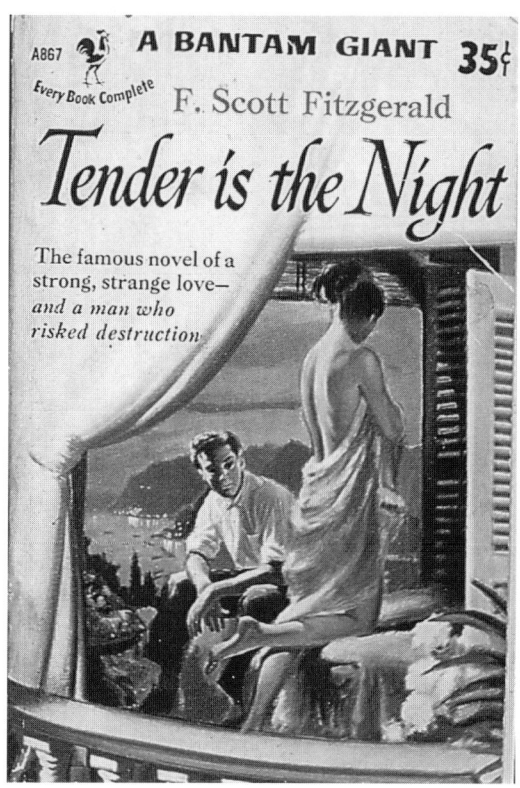

110. *The Great Gatsby* (Harmondsworth: Penguin Books, 1950).

This is the second English edition. Penguin was influential in keeping Fitzgerald's name before readers abroad. *The Great Gatsby* has been on Penguin's list of titles since the company's first printing of it. Later in the decade Penguin added *Tender Is the Night,* then *The Last Tycoon,* and, eventually, other Fitzgerald titles.

111. Charles Scribner's Sons royalty report to Scottie Fitzgerald Lanahan, February 1, 1952.

Scottie Fitzgerald Lanahan, F. Scott Fitzgerald's daughter, received semiannual reports about Fitzgerald's works from Scribners. The reports document sales figures and prices in addition to accounting for other publishers who had leased rights to reprint short stories and novels. This report, from July to December 1951, shows the marked increase in sales that paperback editions produced.

112. Harold Ober Associates summary of income and expenses to Scottie Fitzgerald Lanahan for January–December 1953, dated January 13, 1954.

This report, representative of activity throughout the 1950s, shows the variety of subsidiary rights which generated income from the works of F. Scott Fitzgerald, in addition to the sales of novels and stories. Rights for potential television, play, and screen productions were leased frequently in the years of the revival. The number of foreign-language translations expanded also, as did the number of times rights were leased by other publishers.

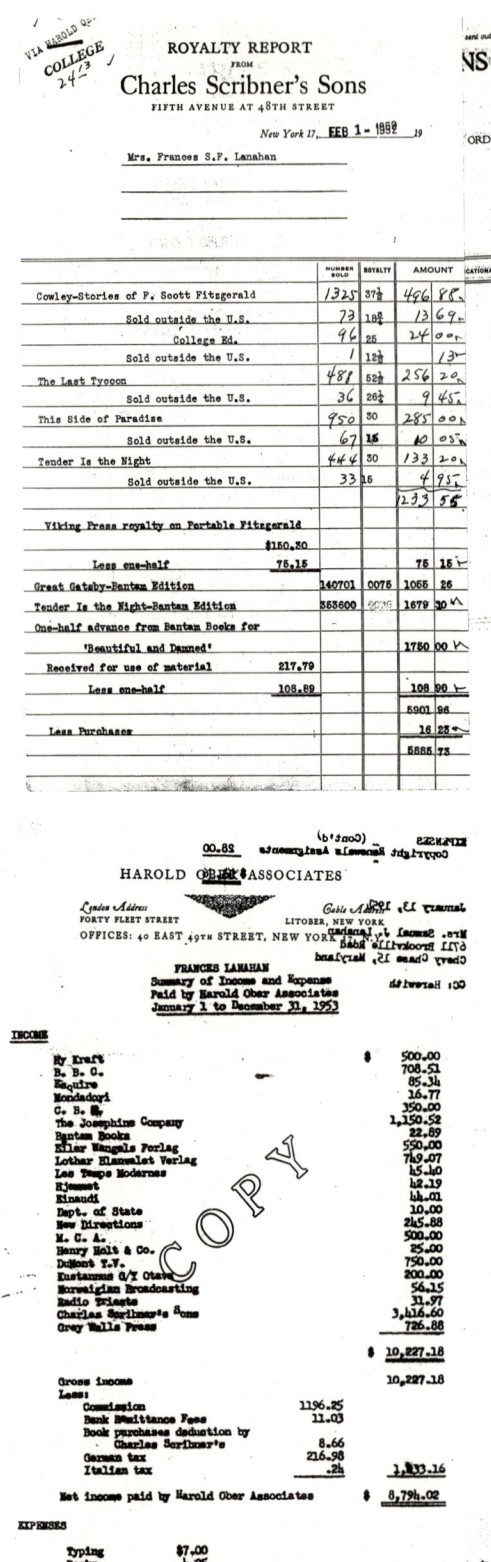

Supplementary Display Cases

by Robert W. Trogdon

SMALL CASES

113. Ernest Boyd, *Portraits: Real and Imaginary* (New York: Doran, [1924]).

Note by Fitzgerald on free front endpaper. Also blind impression of Ernest Hemingway's printing on p. [266]: "MADAME FITZGERALD 14 RUE TILSITT PARIS SCOTT MISSED TRAIN PLEASE WIRE HIM CARE GARAGE I WILL BE AT HOTEL BRISTOL LYON WIRE ME ADDRESS OF GARAGE THERE HEMINGWAY." Hemingway used the rear endpaper of this copy to write a wire when Fitzgerald failed to meet him, an episode described in *A Moveable Feast* (1964).

114. *The Beautiful and Damned* (New York: Scribners, 1922), inscribed to Minneapolis bookseller A. L. Sugarman and notarized August 2, 1922.

115. Fitzgerald to Ben Abramson, March 17, 1936, Baltimore, Md., TLS, 1 p.; Fitzgerald to Argus Book Shop, April 7, 1936, Baltimore, Md., TLS, 1 p.

Fitzgerald incorrectly informed the bookseller that the first printing of *This Side of Paradise* could be identified by the misspelling "Campbell" on p. 46; he then corrected his error and advised Abrahamson to check the dust jacket for printing data.

116. John B. Watson, *Behaviorism* (New York: Norton, [1925]), inscribed by Fitzgerald to Anthony D. Sayre.

Judge Sayre, of the Alabama Supreme Court, was Fitzgerald's father-in-law. Fitzgerald sought his respect, as indicated by this inscription.

117. *Tender Is the Night* (London: Chatto & Windus, 1934), proof copy.

The only located proof copy for the British edition of Fitzgerald's fourth novel.

118. Joseph Conrad, *Victory* (Garden City, N.Y. & Toronto: Doubleday, Page, 1921).

Fitzgerald checked the list of Conrad's works on the card page, apparently to indicate those he had read. Conrad was a literary hero to Fitzgerald, who wrote John Peale Bishop on 2 April 1934, " I keep thinking of Conrad's *Nigger of the Narcissus* Preface—and I believe that the important thing about a work of fiction is that the essential reaction shall be profound and enduring" (*Life in Letters*, p. 252).

119. Edmund Wilson, *Poets, Farewell!* (New York: Scribners, 1929), inscribed by Wilson to F. Scott and Zelda Fitzgerald.

Wilson was Fitzgerald's friend from their Princeton years. Fitzgerald identified Edna St. Vincent Millay as the subject of the first section of "Three Women Remembered in Absence."

Large Cases

Upright Case One

120. Portraits of F. Scott and Zelda Fitzgerald by Gordon Bryant, 1920. (Arlyn Bruccoli Collection) See color insert.

121. Fitzgerald's Briefcase. The goldstamped address is that of Charles Scribner's Sons, Fitzgerald's publisher. See color insert.

122. Fitzgerald's Flask.
A gift from Montgomery friends to Fitzgerald before he left Camp Sheridan. The inscription is "M. Edgerton M. Sayre / To / 1st Lt. F. Scott Fitzgerald / 65th Infantry / Camp Sheridan / For-get-me-not / Zelda / 9·13·18 / Montgomery, Ala." See color insert.

123. Fitzgerald's Walking Stick.
A gift from Fitzgerald's editor at Scribners, Maxwell Perkins. On May 12, 1927, Fitzgerald acknowledged receipt, writing Perkins, "The cane was marvelous. The nicest one I ever saw and *infinitely* superior to the one mislaid. Need I say I value the inscription? This is the cane I shall never lose" (*Dear Scott/Dear Max*, pp. 147–148).

124. *St. Paul Daily Dirge* (January 13, 1922). Written and published by Fitzgerald as a joke for distribution at a dance. One of four located copies.

Upright Cases Two and Three

125. Eight Paintings and Drawings by Francis Cugat.
These sketches represent Cugat's preliminary work for the jacket of *The Great Gatsby* and the artist's own copy of the final jacket art. See item 21 and color insert. (Arlyn Bruccoli Collection)

Upright Case Four

126. Class photo, Princeton '17. Signed on verso by many members of the class, including Fitzgerald.

Wall Display: Graniteville Room

by Robert W. Trogdon

127. Fitzgerald's certificate of membership in the National Society of the Children of the American Revolution (September 1, 1903).

128. Fitzgerald as a showgirl in the Princeton Triangle Club's production of "The Evil Eye" (1915). The photograph was published in several newspapers, including *The New York Times* (January 2, 1916).

129. Fitzgerald's passport (1917). Fitzgerald had planned to accompany Monsignor Cyril Sigourney Webster Fay on a diplomatic mission to Russia.

130. Fitzgerald's commission as a second lieutenant in the infantry of the United States Army, October 26, 1917.

131. Fitzgerald's patron card from the Louisville (Kentucky) Free Public Library, 1918. He was in the 45th Infantry Regiment at nearby Camp Zachary Taylor.

132. Still from *The Husband Hunter* (Fox, 1920), the movie version of Fitzgerald's story "Myra Meets His Family" (1920). See item 50.

133. Poster for *The Offshore Pirate* (Metro, 1921), the third movie based on a Fitzgerald work (see item 51 and color insert).

134. Fitzgerald to Carl Winston, c. January 1926, Paris, ALS, 1 p. Winston was a reporter who met Fitzgerald at Bricktop's, a Paris nightclub; the letter mentions Jay Gatsby.

135. Fitzgerald's check to Collector of Internal Revenue (March 15, 1929) for $227.28.

136. Edward Shenton's original art for *Tender Is the Night* (1934). Shenton's pen-and-ink decorations were commissioned for the *Scribner's Magazine* serial and retained in the book (see item 23).

137. Inscription to Laura Guthrie removed from *Tender Is the Night* (New York: Scribners, 1934). This inscription to Fitzgerald's secretary in Asheville, N.C., during 1935–1936 stipulates a 1917–1930 time frame for the novel; but 1929 is the likelier terminus ad quem.

138. Poster for *Three Comrades* (M-G-M, 1938), the only movie for which Fitzgerald received screen credit (see item 82). See color insert.

139. Poster for *The Great Gatsby* (Paramount, 1949), with Alan Ladd as Jay Gatsby (see item 103). See color insert.

140. Original *Peanuts* art by Charles Schulz (July 22, 1990; June 7, 1991; December 18, 1991), inscribed by the artist. These panels refer to Jay Gatsby.

141. Don Swann, engraving of The Elms, home of Francis Scott Key, inscribed to F. Scott Fitzgerald. (Arlyn Bruccoli Collection)

142. Zelda Fitzgerald, decorated wooden dish with a transportation motif printed in oil. (Arlyn Bruccoli Collection)

143. Zelda Fitzgerald, gouache illustration of "The Lobster Quadrille" from *Alice in Wonderland*. See color insert. (Arlyn Bruccoli Collection)

144. Zelda Fitzgerald, gouache painting of flowers. (Arlyn Bruccoli Collection)

145. Zelda Fitzgerald, signed gouache painting of flowers in bowl. (Arlyn Bruccoli Collection)

146. Zelda Fitzgerald, oil painting of flowers. (Arlyn Bruccoli Collection)

147. Zelda Fitzgerald, block printing of torso; used as greeting card by the Fitzgeralds. (Arlyn Bruccoli Collection)

148. Zelda Fitzgerald, gouache painting of dancers. See color insert. (Arlyn Bruccoli Collection)

149. F. Scott Fitzgerald, map of France drawn for Scottie Fitzgerald.

150. Drawing of Sylvia Beach by Stephen Longstreet. (Arlyn Bruccoli Collection)

151. Advertising card for Shakespeare and Company.

Apprenticeship: St. Paul Academy, Newman School, and Princeton University, 1909–1917

by Robert W. Trogdon

By the time Fitzgerald wrote his first novel he had served a nine-year apprenticeship by writing for the literary journals at his schools and university. At Princeton he neglected his studies to write for the *Nassau Lit*, the *Princeton Tiger*, and the Triangle Club.

152. "The Mystery of the Raymond Mortgage," *The St. Paul Academy Now and Then* **(October 2, 1909).**

Fitzgerald's first publication; he had five by-lined appearances in *Now and Then*.

153. Fitzgerald's Report Card from Newman School, January 1912.

Like most literary geniuses, Fitzgerald was indifferent to the attractions of mathematics and science.

154. "A Luckless Santa Claus," *Newman News* **(Christmas 1912).**

Fitzgerald's first story in his prep-school magazine. The Christmas 1912 issue also included a photo of the football team with halfback Fitzgerald.

155. "Martin's Thoughts," MS, 1 p., c. 1913, and untitled poem, MS, 1 p., c. 1914.

Presumably the earliest surviving manuscripts of Fitzgerald's verse. The subject of "Martin's Thoughts" is Martin Amorous, his prep-school friend.

156. *Fie! Fie! Fi-Fi!* [Princeton Triangle Club, 1914].

The acting script for Fitzgerald's first Triangle Club show written during his freshman year: one of two known copies and the only one with Fitzgerald's additional printed lyrics.

157. *Fie! Fie! Fi-Fi!* (Cincinnati: John Church, 1914).

This songbook credits Fitzgerald with the plot and lyrics, but he actually wrote the entire book, which was revised by the president of the Triangle Club. See color insert.

158. *The Evil Eye* (Cincinnati: John Church, 1915).

The songbook for Fitzgerald's second Triangle Club show, on which he collaborated with Edmund Wilson, '16—who became Fitzgerald's "intellectual conscience." See color insert.

159. *Safety First!* (Cincinnati: John Church, 1916).

The songbook for Fitzgerald's final Triangle Club show, on which he collaborated with John Biggs, '18—who became chief judge of the U. S. Court of Appeals for the Third Circuit and served as executor of Fitzgerald's estate. See color insert.

160. Fitzgerald and John Biggs, Jr., "Cedric the Stoker," *The Princeton Tiger* (November 10, 1917).

Fitzgerald later claimed that he and John Biggs wrote whole issues of the Princeton humor magazine. Thirty-six of Fitzgerald's *Tiger* contributions—mostly unsigned—have been identified.

161. "Sentiment—and the Use of Rouge," *Nassau Literary Magazine* (June 1917).

This issue of the *Nassau Lit* bears Fitzgerald's handwritten note to Cecilia Taylor ("Cousin Ceci"). Fitzgerald had twenty-five appearances in the *Lit*—nine poems, six stories, two plays, three parodies, and five book reviews—marking the inception of his serious apprenticeship (see item 97).

162. *The Nassau Herald Class of 1917.*

Fitzgerald's class book noted that "He will pursue graduate work in English at Harvard, then he will engage in newspaper work."

163. *The Princeton Bric-A-Brac 1917.*

The university yearbook accorded prominent coverage to *Fie! Fie! Fi-Fi!*

Zelda Fitzgerald

by Robert W. Trogdon and Tracy Simmons Bitonti

Zelda Sayre Fitzgerald created remarkable works as a writer and as a painter. Her wit and her ability to make surprising connections distinguished her prose as authentically individual.

164. Zelda Fitzgerald to Judge and Mrs. A. D. Sayre, c. 1924, postcards.

Most likely from the Fitzgeralds' second trip to Europe in 1924, the cards document Zelda Fitzgerald's devotion to her parents.

165. "The Girl With Talent," *College Humor* (April 1930).

Zelda Fitzgerald began her writing career with light nonfiction articles and also tried the short-story genre. At the magazine's insistence the joint by-line read "by F. Scott and Zelda Fitzgerald."

166. Lubov Egorova to Zelda Fitzgerald, [August] 17, 1929, Neris-les-Bains, postcard.

One of the reasons Zelda Fitzgerald wanted to write short stories was to earn money for her ballet lessons with Egorova, a celebrated teacher in Paris.

167. Four postcards of Les Rives de Prangins, with F. Scott Fitzgerald's notations.

Zelda Fitzgerald suffered her first mental breakdown in April 1930. After hospitalization in Paris she was transferred on June 5 to the Prangins clinic in Nyon, Switzerland.

168. "Miss Ella," *Scribner's Magazine* (December 1931); "A Couple of Nuts," *Scribner's Magazine* (August 1932).

Two of Zelda Fitzgerald's best short stories appeared in the magazine published by Charles Scribner's Sons. "Miss Ella" describes a southern lady who remains a spinster after a former suitor commits suicide. "A Couple of Nuts," her last published story, depicts the deterioration of a married couple who are entertainers in Europe.

169. *Save Me the Waltz* (New York: Scribners, 1932).

Zelda Fitzgerald's only novel is heavily autobiographical, and Fitzgerald was upset by her appropriation of material he intended to develop in *Tender Is the Night*. After she made revisions, Scribners published the novel on October 7. It was not well received; readers and critics had difficulty with Zelda Fitzgerald's idiosyncratic prose style. See color insert.

170. Zelda Fitzgerald, holograph notes about writing, 2 pp.

These notes document Zelda Fitzgerald's use of her husband's writing as a model for her own.

171. *Scandalabra* **(Bloomfield Hills, Mich. & Columbia, S.C.: Bruccoli Clark, 1980).**

This play, billed as "A Farce Fantasy in a Prologue and Three Acts," was Zelda Fitzgerald's last completed writing project. It was performed in a six-night run by the Vagabond Junior Players in Baltimore, Md., at the end of June 1933.

172. "Painting by Zelda Fitzgerald/Photographs by Marion Hines," March 29–April 30, 1934: exhibition catalogue with F. Scott Fitzgerald's notes.

Zelda Fitzgerald's third artistic outlet was painting. Fitzgerald helped to arrange a joint exhibition in New York of her work with photographs by a doctor at John Hopkins Medical School. Fitzgerald listed the friends who attended and bought paintings.

173. Zelda Fitzgerald to Anne Ober, August 12, 1946, Highland Hospital, Asheville, N.C., ALS, 3 pp.

In this letter Zelda Fitzgerald expresses her appreciation for the Obers' continued concern with her welfare and that of Scottie Fitzgerald.

Scripts Based on Fitzgerald's Works

by Paul D. Schultz

F. Scott Fitzgerald's writings have been frequently dramatized by other writers, with mainly indifferent results. The movie versions have been particularly disappointing because literary style is not photographable.

Stage

174. *The Great Gatsby* (1926). Adapted by Owen Davis; directed by George Cukor at the Ambassador Theater, New York City, February 2, 1926.

175. *This Side of Paradise* (1962). Adapted by Sydney Sloane; staged by Herbert Berghof with choreography by J. C. McCord at the Sheridan Stage Theater, New York City, February 21, 1962.

Television

176. *Tender Is the Night* (General Electric Presents Front Row Center, 1955). Adapted by Whitfield Cook; directed by Fletcher Markle.

177. *F. Scott Fitzgerald and "The Last of the Belles"* (ABC, 1974). Script by James Costigan; directed by George Schaefer.

Motion Pictures

178. *Tender Is the Night* (Twentieth Century–Fox, 1962). Final script, January 31, 1961. Adapted by Ivan Moffat; directed by Henry King.

179. *The Great Gatsby* (Paramount, 1974). Revised screenplay, September 7, 1972. Adapted by Francis Ford Coppola; directed by Jack Clayton. See also the 1948 adaptation, item 103.

180. *The Last Tycoon* (Paramount, 1976). Revised screenplay, October 30, 1975. Adapted by Harold Pinter; directed by Elia Kazan.

Scottie Fitzgerald, 1921–1986

The birth certificate for the only child of F. Scott and Zelda Fitgerald stipulates her name as "Scotty," and she was christened Frances Scott Fitzgerald. All of her life she was known as "Scottie." She was a talented writer; her by-line appeared in *The New Yorker*, *The Washington Post*, *The New York Times*, *The Democratic Digest*, and *The Northern Virginia Sun*. She also wrote benefit musicals produced in Washington, D.C., and plays intended for Broadway.

Scottie responsibly and unavariciously performed her duties as custodian of her parents' literary properties. She was patient and generous with students and researchers. Her donation of the F. Scott Fitzgerald Papers to Princeton University in 1950 stimulated and enriched Fitzgerald scholarship.

Matthew J. Bruccoli began working with Scottie in 1969, and they worked together on five "Daddy books." She is greatly mourned.

181. F. Scott Fitzgerald to Scottie, postcards, 1928–1932.

Fitzgerald usually improved the picture postcards he sent Scottie with his own artwork (see item 38). See color insert.

182. Historical postcards, c. 1930.

A lifelong history buff, Fitzgerald endeavored to tutor Scottie in French history by annotating a set of postcards. See color insert.

183. Parental guidance, 1938.

These wires from Fitzgerald in California to Scottie are supplemented by a postcard instructing her how to get the most out of her summer trip to Europe.

184. "The Right Person Won't Write," 1939

Scottie wrote and directed OMGIM (O My God, It's Monday!) shows at Vassar. This song from "Remember the Daze," the class of '42 Sophomore Party, achieved Ivy League popularity.

185. *Taps at Reveille* (New York: Scribners, 1935), inscribed by Scottie to Matthew J. Bruccoli.

Scottie Fitzgerald gave this book to Bruccoli on the occasion of their first meeting, Baltimore, Md., October 9, 1964.

186. "Love Among Other Things," TS, 1964.

None of Scottie's plays made it to Broadway. This satirical treatment of infidelity was her last completed play.

187. *The Romantic Egoists* (New York: Scribners, 1974), Scottie's revised introduction and working notes.

Scottie, Joan Paterson Kerr (her Vassar classmate), and Bruccoli edited this "pictorial autobiography" of F. Scott and Zelda Fitzgerald—working together at the Scribner Building.

188. *Some Sort of Epic Grandeur,* annotated TS.

Scottie vetted the penultimate draft of Bruccoli's *Some Sort of Epic Grandeur* (New York: Harcourt Brace Jovanovich, 1981).

189. "The Colonial Ancestors of Francis Scott Key Fitzgerald," Scottie's revised TS, 20 pp., with genealogies and cover letter to Bruccoli, March 24, 1981.

This is Scottie's revised draft of the appendix she wrote for *Some Sort of Epic Grandeur.*

M.J.B.

Scottie Fitzgerald in front of 6 Pleasant Avenue, Montgomery, Alabama, where her father courted her mother in 1918.

Primary Bibliography

Fie! Fie! Fi-Fi! Cincinnati, New York & London: The John Church Co., 1914.

The Evil Eye. Cincinnati, New York & London: The John Church Co., 1915.

Safety First. Cincinnati, New York & London: The John Church Co., 1916.

This Side of Paradise. New York: Scribners, 1920; London: Collins, 1921.

Flappers and Philosophers. New York: Scribners, 1920; London: Collins, 1922.

The Beautiful and Damned. New York: Scribners, 1922; London: Collins, 1922.

Tales of the Jazz Age. New York: Scribners, 1922; London: Collins, 1923.

The Vegetable. New York: Scribners, 1923.

The Great Gatsby. New York: Scribners, 1925; London: Chatto & Windus, 1926. *The Great Gatsby: A Facsimile of the Manuscript,* ed. Matthew J. Bruccoli. Washington: Bruccoli Clark/NCR Microcard Books, 1973.

All the Sad Young Men. New York: Scribners, 1926.

Tender Is the Night. New York: Scribners, 1934; London: Chatto & Windus, 1934. *Tender Is the Night,* "With the Author's Final Revisions," ed. Malcolm Cowley. New York: Scribners, 1951; London: Grey Walls, 1953.

Taps at Reveille. New York: Scribners, 1935.

The Last Tycoon. New York: Scribners, 1941; London: Grey Walls, 1949. With *The Great Gatsby* and 5 stories.

The Crack-Up, ed. Edmund Wilson. New York: New Directions, 1945.

The Stories of F. Scott Fitzgerald, ed. Malcolm Cowley. New York: Scribners, 1951.

Afternoon of an Author, ed. Arthur Mizener. Princeton, N.J.: Princeton University Library, 1957; New York: Scribners, 1958; London: Bodley Head, 1958.

The Pat Hobby Stories, ed. Arnold Gingrich. New York: Scribners, 1962; Harmondsworth: Penguin, 1967.

The Letters of F. Scott Fitzgerald, ed. Andrew Turnbull. New York: Scribners, 1964; London: Bodley Head, 1964.

The Apprentice Fiction of F. Scott Fitzgerald, ed. John Kuehl. New Brunswick, N.J.: Rutgers University Press, 1965.

Thoughtbook of Francis Scott Key Fitzgerald, ed. John Kuehl. Princeton, N.J.: Princeton University Library, 1965.

F. Scott Fitzgerald in His Own Time: A Miscellany, ed. Matthew J. Bruccoli and Jackson R. Bryer. Kent, Ohio: Kent State University Press, 1971.

Dear Scott/Dear Max, ed. John Kuehl and Jackson R. Bryer. New York: Scribners, 1971; London: Cassell, 1973.

As Ever, Scott Fitz—, ed. Matthew J. Bruccoli and Jennifer M. Atkinson. Philadelphia and New York: Lippincott, 1972; London: Woburn, 1973.

The Basil and Josephine Stories, ed. Jackson R. Bryer and John Kuehl. New York: Scribners, 1973.

F. Scott Fitzgerald's Ledger (A Facsimile), ed. Matthew J. Bruccoli. Washington: Bruccoli Clark/NCR Microcard Books, 1973.

Bits of Paradise, ed. Matthew J. Bruccoli and Scottie Fitzgerald Smith. London: Bodley Head, 1973; New York: Scribners, 1974.

F. Scott Fitzgerald's Screenplay for Eric Maria Remarque's Three Comrades, ed. Matthew J. Bruccoli. Carbondale & Edwardsville: Southern Illinois University Press, 1978.

The Notebooks of F. Scott Fitzgerald, ed. Matthew J. Bruccoli. New York & London: Harcourt Brace Jovanovich/Bruccoli Clark, 1978.

F. Scott Fitzgerald's St. Paul Plays, ed. Alan Margolies. Princeton, N.J.: Princeton University Library, 1978.

The Price Was High, ed. Matthew J. Bruccoli. New York & London: Harcourt Brace Jovanovich/Bruccoli Clark, 1979; London: Quartet, 1979.

Correspondence of F. Scott Fitzgerald, ed. Matthew J. Bruccoli and Margaret M. Duggan, with Susan Walker. New York: Random House, 1980.

Poems 1911–1940, ed. Matthew J. Bruccoli. Bloomfield Hills, Mich. & Columbia, S.C.: Bruccoli Clark, 1981.

The Short Stories of F. Scott Fitzgerald, ed. Matthew J. Bruccoli. New York: Scribners, 1989; London: Scribners, 1991.

Babylon Revisited: The Screenplay, intro. Budd Schulberg. New York: Carroll & Graf, 1993.

F. Scott Fitzgerald: A Life In Letters, ed. Matthew J. Bruccoli, with Judith S. Baughman. New York: Scribners, 1994.

F. Scott Fitzgerald on Authorship, ed. Matthew J. Bruccoli, with Judith S. Baughman. Columbia: University of South Carolina Press, 1996.

Facsimile Volumes

F. Scott Fitzgerald Manuscripts, ed. Matthew J. Bruccoli. New York & London: Garland, 1990–1991. 18 vols.: *This Side of Paradise, The Beautiful and Damned, The Great Gatsby* galleys, *Tender Is the Night, The Vegetable,* stories, and articles.

Critical Editions

The Cambridge Edition of the Works of F. Scott Fitzgerald. Cambridge, New York, Port Chester, Melbourne, Sydney: Cambridge University Press, 1991– . 15 vols. projected. *The Great Gatsby,* ed. Matthew J. Bruccoli (1991); *The Love of the Last Tycoon: A Western,* ed. Matthew J. Bruccoli (1992).

Tender Is the Night: A Romance, ed. Matthew J. Bruccoli. London: Everyman, 1996

Secondary Bibliography

Berg, A. Scott. *Max Perkins: Editor of Genius.* New York: Dutton, 1978.

Bruccoli, Matthew J. *F. Scott Fitzgerald: A Descriptive Bibliography, Revised Edition.* Pittsburgh: University of Pittsburgh Press, 1987.

———. *Fitzgerald and Hemingway: A Dangerous Friendship.* New York: Carroll & Graf, 1994.

———. *Some Sort of Epic Grandeur: The Life of F. Scott Fitzgerald.* Rev. ed., New York: Carroll & Graf, 1991.

——— with Judith S. Baughman. *Reader's Companion to F. Scott Fitzgerald's Tender Is the Night.* Columbia: University of South Carolina Press, 1996.

Dos Passos, John. *The Best Times.* New York: New American Library, 1968.

Graham, Sheilah, and Gerold Frank. *Beloved Infidel.* New York: Holt, 1958.

O'Hara, John. Introduction. *The Portable F. Scott Fitzgerald,* selected by Dorothy Parker. New York: Viking, 1945.

Seldes, Gilbert. "Spring Flight," *F. Scott Fitzgerald: The Critical Reception,* ed. Jackson Bryer (New York: Burt Franklin, 1978), pp. 239–241.

Smith, Scottie Fitzgerald. "Notes About My Now-Famous Father." *Family Circle,* 84 (May 1974), pp. 118–120.

Smith, Scottie Fitzgerald, Matthew J. Bruccoli, and Joan P. Kerr, eds. *The Romantic Egoists: A Pictorial Autobiography from the Scrapbooks and Albums of F. Scott and Zelda Fitzgerald.* New York: Scribners, 1974.